MW01600650

Enough Time Your 90-day devotion

By

Angela Denise Boston

Enough Time – Your 90-day devotion™
Author: Angela Denise Boston ©2023

All rights reserved. No part of this book may be reproduced, stored in a retrievable system, scanned, electronically, mechanically, digitally transmitted, photocopied in any form by any means, or distributed in any printed or electronic form without the written permission of the publisher or author Angela Denise Boston.

Please do not participate in or encourage piracy of copyrighted materials in violation of the author's rights.

Please purchase only authorized copies or editions of this book.
Order books directly from the author or approved sellers.

Unless otherwise noted all scriptures are from the following translations of the HOLY BIBLE:
King James Version (**KJV**), New King James Version (**NKJV**), New Living Translation (**NLT**), English Standard Version (**ESV**), New International Version (**NIV**), American Standard Version (**ASV**), Good News Translation (**GNT**), God Word (**GW**)

Contact **Boston Enterprises** for more information or to request the author's participation in any speaking engagements, ministry events, bible studies, teambuilding, class trainings, or any special events.

Make special event request for the author *Angela Denise Boston* **at the following**:
BOSTON ENTERPRISES™
P.O. Box 29271
Dallas, TX 75220
bostonenterprises@att.net
office: (214) 366-3638

Printed in the United States of America

Graphic Design and Book Cover: Osato Agboaye and Monica Robinson
Book Editors: Jill Westberry, Erin King, and Gwen Hart
Picture of Author and Makeup: Pretty Beat By Tek - Antequa Chatman

About the Author

1 Timothy 1:12 (KJV) *"And I thank Christ Jesus our LORD who hath enabled me, for that he counted me faithful putting me into the ministry."*

As a chosen, anointed vessel of GOD, Angela began answering the call into ministry in August 1998 and gave an Absolute Surrender "Yes" to the Heavenly Father in March 2003 under the leadership of Evangelist Gwen Hart of Women Reaching Women Ministries. In August 2005, Angela was Ordained and Licensed under the pastoral covering of Senior Pastor Cedric D. Jackson at Love Fellowship Family Church. At the time of authoring this book, Angela works in both Academia and Corporate America. Angela is also caregiver to both her parents Wilbert Boston and Marietta Moffitt. Angela currently resides in Dallas, TX and has 1 adult daughter—Antequa.

Angela's education includes having an MBA in Strategic Leadership (Human Resources), a Bachelor's degree in Business Administration (Management), and also an Associate degree in Liberal arts. Her work experience includes having a wealth of 30+ years of direct HR leadership experience supporting multi-states, regions, districts, field locations and support shared services departments, with a variety of prominent companies in the United States which includes directing and developing high performing HR teams of professionals, company leaders, and front-line managers. Angela also has served over 19+ years teaching Human Resources course work at prominent Universities, which includes several years full-time in the College of Business for The University of Texas at Arlington and now currently, as a part-time Adjunct Faculty in the School of Business for the University of North Texas on the Dallas campus. As a prominent leader in her profession, Angela Denise Boston has been recognized by Cambridge Who's Who Among Executives and

Professionals as well as Who's Who Among American Teachers, and Who's Who in Business Higher Education. In addition, Angela is the owner and principal consultant of Boston Enterprises and is a member of Delta Sigma Theta Sorority, Inc.

Angela summarizes her ministry journey and personal testimony as follows: "BUT GOD! —For I thank you GOD the Heavenly Father, Son, and Holy Spirit for loving me, forgiving me, saving me, cleansing me, filling me, and using me for GOD's Glory, Honor, and Praise. For you LORD GOD always knew THE PLAN you had for me! To GOD BE the GLORY forever, and ever AMEN!"

Onward and Upward with no limits and no boundaries!

--- Angela D. Boston

DEDICATIONS:

To GOD
This one is for you—because of you!
I simply say:
For GOD, By GOD, Through Angela Denise Boston
It is my dedicated first fruit
Thank you LORD for being the 1st to love me!

To all the people that GOD had in mind
who say they don't have
Enough Time!

ACKNOWLEDGEMENTS

I would like to acknowledge the following people for their continual support, prayers, and encouragement throughout this process to complete this project:

My Grandmother – Mable Roy Boston. Continue to root for me and cheer me on from Heaven! When no one else thought I could, you <u>always knew</u> I would! I thank GOD for the prayers of my grandmother spoken over my life. Bigmama taught me early about GOD and instilled and cultivated my faith belief. Priceless!

My parents – Wilbert Boston & Marietta Moffitt you were used to get me in the earth to IMPACT the world! I am truly blessed to still have you both present with me to celebrate this moment in time achievement. Who would have ever thought the roles would be reversed and you would now be my Parent-kids. It is an honor and privilege to care for you both at this stage of your life! It's been hard, eventful, but yet satisfying.

I want to pause for cause and send a Shout Out of a BIG THANK YOU **to all the caregivers** out there! I pray for you!! May you be recognized and appreciated for being the "unsung heroes" that you are! Much Love!

My daughter—Antequa Lynn Chatman you have had a front row seat in my life. Thank you for stepping up when I needed you most and being able to see me in my valleys and the peaks experiencing the good, bad, and indifferent phases of my life's journey. The <u>ultimate</u> BEST is YET to COME! For GOD knows THE PLAN!

Evangelist Gwen Hart and Pastor Betty White - there are no words that can express my love and appreciation for you both. GOD anointed & appointed – PERIOD.

My writing squad—Rev. Monica Robinson and Dr. Cecilia D. Wilson Smith thank you both for pushing me from the beginning, even when I tried to make an excuse that the 2019 tornadoes took my book notes. GOD used you both to say, "show up" & "get started."

Osato Agboaye – My GOD appointed son. Who would have ever thought that the first day you walked into my class "late" with your hat turned to the back dressed in all white (angel unaware), you were sent for a lifetime and not just for that semester. Much Love Always!

All others – Family, Friends, Sorority Sisters, Bishops, Pastors, Ministry groups, Students, Colleagues, and Corporate leaders who have invested time, energy, knowledge, experiences, resources, and encouragement during an encounter with me, Thank you!

To: THE READER

Thank You!
For taking some **Time**

We all get 24 hours & 7-days a week of Time
Each of us choose
what we will do in that Time

I have lived moments in Time that could be classified in
categories of:
A Matter of Time, Granted Time, In the Nic of Time, and now
Enough Time!

In this short span of dedicated Time,

My sincere prayer and hope is
that you will be
Blessed, Encouraged, Challenged and Strengthen
by the words
that shall flow from these pages.

Thanks again!
For investing your valuable Time
into

Enough Time
Your 90-day devotion.

TABLE OF CONTENTS

INTRODUCTION

Life has so many demands, obligations, and necessities that require our time and attention that in only a matter of time we may find ourselves not taking some time to nourish our own need to be invigorated, stimulated, refreshed, cheered, and reassured.

When faced with these challenges, one WORD and a quick PRAYER can go a long way in helping us through the day.

Over the next 90-days, let this *pause* for *this cause* be just that for you!

Enough Time.

Day 1 – ENDURANCE

Hebrews 12: 1-2 (NLT) *"Therefore since we are surrounded by such a huge crowd of witnesses to the life of faith, let us strip off every weight that slows us down, especially the sin that so easily trips us up. And let us run with endurance the race GOD has set before us."*

❖ What gets me through each day when faced with multiple demands? Endurance!

When examining the word ENDURANCE, it is the capacity of something or someone to last or withstand wear and tear or an event that takes place over a long period of time that demands great spiritual and physical stamina. ENDURANCE also means the ability to last.

One main aspect of ENDURANCE denotes "TIME" and that being for a long period of it. Time is the very thing we may say we don't have because of the lack of properly knowing HOW TO plan and prioritize. ENDURANCE also takes exercising the foundations of hope, faith, and belief. We must believe that what it is we are *going through* or *going to do* will be well worth it in the end. If we don't – we simply won't! ENDURE.

Endure to the end my friend!

Remember that you have a race to run and a certain time to do it in. Only GOD knows the beginning time and the end time. Let's seek Him!

PRAYER:
Thank you LORD for already knowing the beginning and the end. I ask that you order my day and my steps along the way. For only I can accomplish that which you have set before me this day. GOD let your will be done! Provide me the Endurance that is needed. In Jesus Name —
Amen!

ENDURANCE

MY NOTES:

_____
_____
_____
_____
_____
_____
_____
_____
_____
_____
_____
_____
_____
_____
_____

ENDURANCE

MY PRAYER:

_____
_____
_____
_____
_____
_____
_____
_____
_____
_____
_____
_____

Day 2—CARE

1 Peter 5:7 (NLT) *"Give all your worries and cares to GOD for he cares about you."*

❖ What would it really be like to have no cares?

When examining the word CARE, it is the provision of what is necessary for the health, welfare, maintenance, and protection of someone or something. CARE also means giving serious attention to or attaching importance to something or someone.

It is amazing to try and understand what we choose to really CARE about or CARE for. Many times, if the person, situation, circumstance, or event does not have a personal impact on us directly, we can easily tend to not care. Let us take a look at this very moment of your life and ask --- What do I care about?? It is the very people, places, or things that you are attaching importance to and giving serious attention to at this time in your life. Now ask—Am I giving that same importance and attention to myself?? Are these things equivalent or do some adjustments truly need to be made?

Self-Care is a thing! As a matter of fact, it really is a required action we should all take a moment to examine how we apply this to our own self in several areas: spiritually, mentally, emotionally, physically, financially, and relationally.

Remember there are many people, places, & things that want or desires to demand care from you but it's only one you. We can't be everywhere or even everything to everybody. That is a role and responsibility that belongs to GOD. So, let's take the time to cast <u>ALL</u> our cares and worries upon Him!

PRAYER:
Thank you, LORD, for caring about me! Self-Care does require me to look at the areas in my life that I may not be trusting you fully to provide and guide. I do so now and believe GOD is well able to do all that is needed & required. In Jesus Name – Amen!

CARE

MY NOTES:

_____
_____
_____
_____
_____
_____
_____
_____
_____
_____
_____
_____
_____
_____
_____

CARE

MY PRAYER:

_____
_____
_____
_____
_____
_____
_____
_____
_____
_____
_____
_____
_____
_____

Day 3—HELP

Psalms 121:1-2 (KJV) *"I will lift up mine eyes unto the hills from whence cometh my help. My help cometh from the LORD which made heaven and earth."*

❖ HELP is such a powerful 4 letter word!

When examining the word HELP, signifies aid, support, and to increase the strength of someone or something. HELP is also an action of making it easier by offering one's services or resources. HELP can also be an appeal or cry for urgent assistance.

It may be easier to cry out for HELP when you are in deep trouble or even facing death! Nonetheless, what tends to keep us from seeking, asking, or getting HELP even before it may be needed? Also, if you were given a source of unlimited supply--- would you utilize the source? If not, then why not? If so, then we might ask, "Where can this source of unlimited supply be found?" The direction given is simply--lift up your eyes.

Remember, GOD is a very present HELP in times of trouble. No matter what the issue, situation, or circumstance is that is troubling you or one you may be facing or dealing with--GOD can HELP! Oh, by the way, just in case it is urgent –GOD *still* can HELP! No matter what time of day or night---GOD can HELP! Have you asked GOD for his help? We need to use it more than we have, more than we think, and more than we know.

PRAYER:
Thank you GOD for being a very present HELP for me! I ask that you provide me with the HELP I need in every endeavor. Forgive me for when I have failed to ask for your HELP, even when confident or overwhelmed. Continue to HELP me to ask for your help sooner and to be willing to receive the HELP you send me. In JESUS Name – Amen!

HELP

MY NOTES:

_____
_____
_____
_____
_____
_____
_____
_____
_____
_____
_____
_____
_____
_____

HELP

MY PRAYER:

_____
_____
_____
_____
_____
_____
_____
_____
_____
_____
_____
_____
_____
_____

Day 4—CRY

John 11:35 (KJV) *"Jesus wept."*

❖ Go ahead and CRY—It's ok to do so!

When examining the word CRY, it is to weep or to shed tears. CRY can also be a shout or scream typically to express a powerful feeling or an emotion. In addition, CRY can also be an urgent appeal or entreaty in demanding something as a self-evident requirement or solution.

Reflect and determine when was the last time you cried? Emptying out tears to express our emotions toward a situation or circumstance we have faced or will deal with, does sometime call for a CRY! Even if you consider yourself to be strong and were taught that crying is weak. That is not so! It is a sign of inner strength. Even Jesus wept!

PRAYER:
Thank you LORD for being a perfect example that it IS okay to cry. No matter how easy or hard this expression of emotion may be for me. As I begin to reflect over my life and realize the times that I have cried, wanted to cry, or even failed to cry--I simply take a moment to CRY and know that it is truly okay to do so! In JESUS Name—Amen!

MY NOTES:

_____
_____
_____
_____
_____
_____
_____
_____
_____
_____
_____
_____
_____
_____
_____
_____

MY PRAYER:

_____
_____
_____
_____
_____
_____
_____
_____
_____
_____
_____
_____
_____
_____

Day 5—Just Handle it!

Philippians 4:13 (NKJV) *"I can do all things though Christ who strengthens me."*

❖ You know what to do---What are you waiting for?

When examining some of the reasons we give for why we wait, we are in the act of procrastination. Procrastination is the action of delaying or postponing something. Also, procrastination means to stall, defer, or intentionally delay.

There may be a responsibility, or even a task or duty (pleasant or unpleasant) that just should get done. We may have thought someone else would surely do what was needed and realized the responsibility, task, or duty still remains incomplete and ponder—"Why" is that not done or even "Who" should do it. We may even have our own responsibilities, dreams & goals we hope to attain and still have not moved forward or have intentionally delayed them with our own excuses. Listen to yourself and see what you are currently saying is your reason.

Be a Good Samaritan and no longer pass it by --- Just Handle it!

PRAYER:
Thank you LORD for your patience in the things I have postponed, stalled, made excuses for, or even kept passing by that has really been a form of procrastination. I ask that you give me the understanding I need to really <u>know</u> that I can do all things through Christ because my source of whatever is needed to do comes through Christ and the strength supplied. In JESUS Name—Amen!

JUST HANDLE IT!

MY NOTES:

_____
_____
_____
_____
_____
_____
_____
_____
_____
_____
_____
_____
_____
_____

JUST HANDLE IT!

MY PRAYER:

_____
_____
_____
_____
_____
_____
_____
_____
_____
_____
_____
_____
_____
_____

Day 6—ALONE

Deuteronomy 31: 8 (GNTD) *"The LORD himself will lead you and be with you. He will not fail you or abandon you, so do not lose courage or be afraid."*

❖ Time alone – but never alone.

When examining the word ALONE, it is a state of being on one's own and having no assistance or participation from others. ALONE also means having no one else present.

Relationship and fellowship with other people are essential to mankind. According to the Bible, in the book of Genesis Chapter 2 & 3, In the beginning when GOD decided to make Eve for Adam (NLT 2:18) GOD said, *"It is not good for man to be alone. I will make a helper who is just right for him,"* this denotes an example of two or more people in relationship or fellowship is an essential connection for mankind whether through blood, marriage, a common cause, or even a joint purpose.

Our relationship and fellowship with others can be spiritual, physical, or emotional associations. For example, when GOD was walking in the garden in the cool of the day, The LORD GOD called to Adam and said to him *"Where are you?"* (NKJV 3:9) denotes this as well.

There does come a time when we may find ourselves ALONE. We may even request to "Be ALONE," or decide we need some "ALONE Time." When this occurs, we should understand that ALONE does not mean lonely. The one who created you is still with you!

PRAYER:
Thank you LORD for my personal connection in relationship and fellowship with you! When I realize the moments in my life that being alone is needed or necessary, I must focus to remember and have the faith, trust, and belief –KNOWING that you are with me. In JESUS Name— Amen!

ALONE

MY NOTES:

_____
_____
_____
_____
_____
_____
_____
_____
_____
_____
_____
_____
_____
_____
_____
_____
_____
_____

ALONE

MY PRAYER:

_____
_____
_____
_____
_____
_____
_____
_____
_____
_____
_____
_____
_____
_____

Day 7—WISDOM

Proverb 9:11 (NLT) *"Wisdom will multiply your days and add years to your life."*

❖ Wisdom is the principal thing!

When examining the word WISDOM, it is the quality of having experience, knowledge, and good judgment. It is also the soundness of an action or decision with regard to the application of experience, knowledge, and good judgment.

According to the Bible, the fear of the LORD is the beginning of wisdom (Psalms 111:10). Many times, most people may try to equate wisdom to age. Although there is an element of time that is needed to gain the experience, knowledge, and good judgment, Wisdom is not automatic with older age. The important benefit of Wisdom is best stated in the Word of God.

(*Proverbs 4:5-9 summarized*) "Get wisdom, Get understanding! Do not forget, nor turn away from the words of my mouth. Do not forsake Wisdom, and Wisdom will preserve you; Love Wisdom and Wisdom will keep you. Wisdom is the principal thing; Therefore, get Wisdom. And in all your getting, get understanding. Exalt Wisdom and Wisdom will promote you; Wisdom will bring you honor when you embrace Wisdom. Wisdom will place on your head an ornament of grace, a crown of glory will Wisdom deliver to you."

PRAYER:
Thank you LORD that Wisdom is readily available to me! The bible says if anyone lacks wisdom, let them ASK of GOD that gives to all liberally. Therefore, I ask now for the Wisdom, Knowledge, and Understanding needed in my life, the matters at hand and even my daily activities. I believe I receive WISDOM! In Jesus Name—Amen!

WISDOM

MY NOTES:

_____
_____
_____
_____
_____
_____
_____
_____
_____
_____
_____
_____
_____
_____

WISDOM

MY PRAYER:

_____
_____
_____
_____
_____
_____
_____
_____
_____
_____
_____
_____

Day 8 – Just say "NO"

Matthew 5:37(NKJV) *"But let your YES be yes and your NO be no"*

❖ What can you say NO to today?

When examining the word NO, it is the opposite of yes. No also is a negative answer or decision or can be used in notices to prohibit or reject something specified. In addition, No means hardly any or not at all.

There are times we obligate ourselves to commitments, things, or even people to which we should simply say NO.

The power of "NO" can release you from being overwhelmed and overextended. This is especially true and tried when family or friends are involved. When we look at being a Team player as a part of groups, ministries, organizations, and even the workplace, this also fits. Reflect and see how many times we said YES when we could have simply said NO.

To help you in this process to begin to say NO more, do be reminded of this one thing: We rarely or almost never have to explain our "YES" to someone when given. Therefore, simply put—use and apply the same concept-- We need not explain our NO just like we did not have to explain our YES. The NO said is a decision made--(period)!

PRAYER:
Thank you GOD, for the power to simply say NO to people, places, or things that obligate, overwhelm, and even overextend me in areas that you have given me as a controllable. Let my communications to others be Yes or NO as you deem. In JESUS name—Amen!

JUST SAY "NO"

MY NOTES:

_____
_____
_____
_____
_____
_____
_____
_____
_____
_____
_____
_____
_____
_____
_____

JUST SAY "NO"

MY PRAYER:

_____
_____
_____
_____
_____
_____
_____
_____
_____
_____
_____
_____
_____
_____

Day 9—NEED

Matthew 5:8b (GNTD) *"Your Father already knows what you need before you ask him."*

❖ Your need is <u>NOT</u> a To-Do List!

When examining the word NEED it is something fundamentally required because it is essential or very important. NEED can be a necessity or a circumstance requiring some course of action. NEED also can be a thing that is wanted, required or a state of lacking necessities.

Sure, we all have a need for the basic necessities of food, clothes, shelter, and rest. But to really consider NEED of the entire being for wholeness, we can look at the many examples that Christ has given in the bible when he took time to pray and connect with the Heavenly Father.

No matter whether we choose to pray, meditate, or worship---doing a check-in to recharge your wireless connection to the Divine GOD is a need that has to be fulfilled as well. We would be amazed how much of the other NEEDS we have will get done and met.

Take the time to recognize your own NEED.

PRAYER:
Thank you LORD for being GOD who is well able to meet every need! For you oh GOD already know what I have need of before I ask. At this very moment, I pause and recharge to make a wireless connection to you in prayer. There are times I may overlook the need to do this. I desire to ensure I connect with you to recognize all my needs and believe GOD to continues to give me what I need. In JESUS name—Amen!

NEED

MY NOTES:

_____
_____
_____
_____
_____
_____
_____
_____
_____
_____
_____
_____
_____
_____
_____
_____

NEED

MY PRAYER:

_____
_____
_____
_____
_____
_____
_____
_____
_____
_____
_____
_____
_____
_____
_____

Day 10—Be ENCOURAGED!

1 Samuel 30:6 (KJV) *"And David was greatly distressed; for the people spake of stoning him, because the soul of all the people was grieved, every man for his sons and for his daughters: but David encouraged himself in the LORD his GOD."*

❖ Encourage yourself!

When examining the word ENCOURAGE it is to give confidence, support, or hope to someone. It also means to stimulate or raise levels of interest or activity in someone or something.

There are times when we are faced with difficulties. Even when life situations seem bleak, and we are at a point that we are looking for something or someone to be the "pick me up" needed to brighten the day. Often time, others may be busy with life's pressures and demand so it could seem as if no one is there or available. This is the time that seeking inner strength from GOD will be necessary and the use of positive affirmations and declarations will be required.

Encourage yourself! Start by shifting your focus on all that actually *is good* and *already going right* instead of looking at whatever is not. Simply understand that everything that is *not* ALL RIGHT is still *Alright!*

BE Encouraged!

PRAYER:
Thank you LORD for you are the lifter of my head. When I think of the goodness of what you have already done for me, I can muster up a mustard seed of faith to have the hope to know ---THIS TOO SHALL PASS and ALL SHALL BE WELL. In JESUS Name—Amen!

BE ENCOURAGED!

MY NOTES:

_____
_____
_____
_____
_____
_____
_____
_____
_____
_____
_____
_____
_____
_____
_____
_____

BE ENCOURAGED!

MY PRAYER:

_____
_____
_____
_____
_____
_____
_____
_____
_____
_____
_____
_____
_____
_____

Day 11 – Built Up or Beat Down

Colossians 2:7 (ASV) *"Rooted and built up in him, and established in your faith, even as ye were taught, abounding in thanksgiving."*

❖ Inspired or Tired

When we examine the word phrase being Built Up or Beat Down we will usually look at how we are physically or emotionally feeling at the time. Inspired or Tired.

There is a different perspective that comes in the form of an emotional impact. Let's ask ourselves a question, "How do people walk away feeling once they have encountered you?" Inspired or Tired, Optimistic or Pessimistic, Encourage or Discouraged. A flicker of light or dismal dark?

What truly is your impact on others after an encounter with you? Do you build up or beat down?

PRAYER:
Thank you GOD for being a sure foundation and the light of the world. I pray that when anyone encounters me, that it will be impactful in a way that is inspiring, optimistic, and encouraging. Also, that I can be a light that others can see GOD in and through me. Heighten my awareness and sensitivity toward each of them to build up and not beat down. In JESUS Name—Amen!

BUILT UP or BEAT DOWN

MY NOTES:

_____
_____
_____
_____
_____
_____
_____
_____
_____
_____
_____
_____
_____
_____
_____

BUILT UP or BEAT DOWN

MY PRAYER:

_____
_____
_____
_____
_____
_____
_____
_____
_____
_____
_____
_____
_____
_____

Day 12—LOVE

1 John 4:10-12 (NLT) *"This is real love—not that we loved GOD, but that HE loved us and sent his Son as a sacrifice to take away our sins. Dear friends, since GOD loved us that much, we surely out to love each other.*

❖ LOVE is the Real Thing!

When examining the word LOVE, it is the presence of deep affection and intense interest and pleasure. Love is also defined in choice and actions we make and take. According to the Bible ---GOD is Love!

The word LOVE has been utilized in many different ways to describe many different things in such a way that the depth of its meaning has become questionable in today society's use of it. Nevertheless, if we really exam the LOVE chapter in the Bible is says: *1 Corinthian 4-8a (GW) "Love is patient. Love is kind. Love isn't jealous. It doesn't sing its own praises. It isn't arrogant. It isn't rude. It doesn't think about itself. It isn't irritable. It doesn't keep track of wrongs. It isn't happy when injustice is done, but it is happy with the truth. Love never stops being patient, never stops believing, never stops hoping, never gives up. Love never comes to an end."*

LOVE really is a GOD thing! Let's seek him..

PRAYER:
Thank you GOD for being LOVE and showing us all LOVE for real! GOD, you are the example of what love really looks like. I pray today that I continue to strive to become a walking, talking example of your real, true, and powerful LOVE. In JESUS Name—Amen!

LOVE

MY NOTES:

_____
_____
_____
_____
_____
_____
_____
_____
_____
_____
_____
_____
_____
_____
_____
_____

LOVE

MY PRAYER:

_____
_____
_____
_____
_____
_____
_____
_____
_____
_____
_____
_____

Day 13 – WARRIOR

Judges 6:12 (NIV) *"When the angel of the LORD appeared to Gideon, he said, 'The LORD is with you, might warrior."*

❖ The battle is not yours to fight

When examining the word WARRIOR, it is a brave or experienced soldier or fighter who perseveres or endeavors vigorously to win. Also, WARRIOR is one who does not easily give in or admit defeat despite difficulties or opposition.

There are many battles that come our way in a variety of forms (battles such as in our faith, family, finances, relationships, including mental, emotional, and physical health) that we engage in that we find ourselves weary, tired, or even drained from its continuation.

Nonetheless, have we really asked the questions that even the Mighty warrior David asked in 1 Samuel 30:8 ----Shall I pursue? Shall I overtake?" before we engage the time, money, resources, and efforts. Asking the inquiry questions helps us to pause for the cause to really determine input and outcome.

GOD is Jehovah Nissi and master of all warriors! Thus, the battle really is not ours as warriors, it is the LORD's.

Let's inquire of Him.

PRAYER:
Thank you LORD for being my battle fighter even when I may have engaged in battles or wars that I was not to personally pursue. Help me to inquire of you more to receive the strategy for input and outcome of any battles that I face. Knowing you are with me simply awaiting me to pursue you and not the battle itself. The battle is not mine to fight—it is the LORD. In JESUS Name—Amen!

WARRIOR

MY NOTES:

_____
_____
_____
_____
_____
_____
_____
_____
_____
_____
_____
_____
_____
_____
_____
_____

WARRIOR

MY PRAYER:

_____
_____
_____
_____
_____
_____
_____
_____
_____
_____
_____
_____
_____
_____

Day 14—PRAY

1 Thessalonians 5:17 (NLT) *"Never stop praying."*

❖ Pray-- it really can change things!

When examining the word PRAY it is a verbal or non-verbal act of communication with a deity of worship. PRAY also can be a serious request made or an expression of thanks given by or to someone. In addition, PRAY can be a preface to a request and/or instructions needed.

Praying is universal in all cultures and ethnicities. The method in which we do PRAY and to whom is what differs. However, what seems to be a common underlining foundation when anyone prays is the need, desire, and belief that something will happen or something and/or someone can change the situation, circumstances, person, place, or thing. Also, there is an element of faith in the act of when we pray that hopes or believes the divine deity can do what has been requested.

As for me and my house, prayer is a very *necessary* timeless, effective, and powerful wireless communication to the Almighty GOD to whom is my GOD, my LORD, and my Savior.

So, I ask – Are you living your best life yet or could getting an upgrade in your wireless communication result in a more effective one?

Let us PRAY.

PRAYER:
Thank you LORD for hearing me as I pray and for being attentive to even my groans when I am unable to utter a word. Help me to begin establishing a more consistent and effective lifestyle of prayer in an effort to connect with you LORD GOD for the necessities needed, desired, and hoped for daily. In JESUS Name—Amen!

PRAY

MY NOTES:

_____
_____
_____
_____
_____
_____
_____
_____
_____
_____
_____
_____
_____
_____
_____
_____

PRAY

MY PRAYER:

_____
_____
_____
_____
_____
_____
_____
_____
_____
_____
_____
_____
_____
_____
_____

Day 15 – CHANGE

Malachi 3:6a (KJV) *"For I the LORD, I change not."*

❖ Change is a constant

When examining the word CHANGE it is the act or instance of making or becoming different. It means to transform or be converted from one state, form, or substance into another. It also means to begin to "BE."

Typically, most people do not easily nor readily CHANGE. Routines and habits are a comfort zone for many and when there is an interruption to that routine or habit, there is an emotional response on how it is processed. Either we ignore, deny, or resist change that occurs and rarely do we simply embrace change.

The transformational process of CHANGE when making or becoming different to convert can be a bit painful, but most often will bring about a better result or outcome. We must keep our focus on a constant while we are processing change. GOD is well able to be that constant. With GOD being the constant we need, we can then *Expect* change, *Seek* change, *Embrace* change, and *Manage* change with an expected end to be better.

Ask yourself a few questions:
1. How am I changing?
2. What currently needs to change?

Remember that CHANGE is a *thang*!
So, will you...CHANGE?

PRAYER:
Thank you LORD GOD for being the master change agent who sets in motions the transformation process in my life. No matter what is changing or even how it is changing, LORD you change not! I ask for the endurance, strength, and ability to accept and embrace change with an expectation in GOD that the process will be a better result for me and those impacted by the change. In JESUS Name—Amen!

CHANGE

MY NOTES:

_____
_____
_____
_____
_____
_____
_____
_____
_____
_____
_____
_____
_____
_____

CHANGE

MY PRAYER:

_____
_____
_____
_____
_____
_____
_____
_____
_____
_____
_____
_____
_____

Day 16 – MINDSET

Ephesians 4:23 (KJV) *"And be renewed in the spirit of your mind."*

❖ What are you thinking?

When examining the word MINDSET, it is a settled way of thinking or feeling about someone or something, typically reflected in their attitude and behavior. MINDSET is also an established set of thoughts and conduct held by and shown toward someone or something.

Personal transformation begins with renewing our mind, thoughts, and beliefs about ourselves and other things. Romans 12:2 states we are "transformed by the renewing of our minds." Much of what we think or feel starts in our thoughts and then depending on how often we think on a thing, it becomes a mind-set or a belief.

Many times, if we fail to capture the thought(s) that enters our mind and really assess, explore, inspect, and check it, —whether good, bad, or indifferent— that thought(s) can lead to an error in judgment, decisions, and or behavior. Thus, to renew your MINDSET will require you to think and respond "differently," no longer repeating the old thoughts and actions but really changing to think and do something you never thought or done before—consistently when the old thought or action surfaces.

PRAYER:
Thank you LORD for being GOD the potter that can change the clay. I ask that my mind be renewed in your spirit so that all my attitude, thoughts, beliefs, and actions will be transformed into whom I trust I am created to be according to your good, acceptable, and perfect will for my life. In JESUS Name—Amen!

MINDSET

MY NOTES:

_____
_____
_____
_____
_____
_____
_____
_____
_____
_____
_____
_____
_____
_____

MINDSET

MY PRAYER:

_____
_____
_____
_____
_____
_____
_____
_____
_____
_____
_____
_____
_____

Day 17—TAKE INVENTORY

Psalms 51:6a (KJV) *"Behold, thou desirest truth in the inward parts."*

❖ What are you still holding on to?

When examining the word TAKE INVENTORY it is the action of making a complete list of what is found. It also means to account for goods in stock or contents of a building.

When pursuing a godly life of righteousness in GOD, remember that <u>no sin</u> is too great <u>to be forgiven by GOD</u>. With that said, we need to TAKE INVENTORY of our lives and really determine the truth within regarding if there are any people, places, or things that need not to continue to be a part of our daily living. Also ask the question – Am I holding on to something or someone that GOD has said "NO" to??

We may have made some choices & decisions that resulted in dealing with consequences that we want to rid ourselves of—if this is so, just stop, utilize the moment, and TAKE INVENTORY. GOD can and will forgive us of any sin. Nonetheless, GOD may use the very consequences we are experiencing to get us to the desired state or place needed.

PRAYER:
Thank you LORD GOD for allowing me this moment to TAKE INVENTORY. I pray to be cleansed from within and create in me a clean heart & spirit so that right thoughts, desires, and decisions can result. In JESUS Name—Amen!

TAKE INVENTORY

MY NOTES:

_____
_____
_____
_____
_____
_____
_____
_____
_____
_____
_____
_____
_____
_____
_____
_____

TAKE INVENTORY

MY PRAYER:

_____
_____
_____
_____
_____
_____
_____
_____
_____
_____
_____
_____
_____
_____

Day 18—Yes! LORD

2 Corinthians 1:18-20 (NIV) *"But as surely as GOD is faithful, our message to you is not "Yes" and "No." For the Son of GOD, Jesus Christ, who was preached among you by us—by me and Silas, and Timothy—was not "Yes" and "No," but in him it has always been "Yes." For no matter how many promises GOD has made, they are "Yes" in Christ."*

❖ When you say YES to GOD – HE says YES too….

When examining the word phrase YES! LORD it is an expression of delight. It means to give an affirmative response, answer, or decision. It also means to indicate an expectation of agreement.

As we build a personal relationship with GOD, individually you will discover His faithfulness to His WORD and Promises. The required action for us, individually, is to trust Him while having the faith to believe for the manifestation. While doing so, we will need to realize that during the process--that actual thing, situation, or circumstances may *look* like, *smell* like, and even *sound* like defeat or that a "NO Way" Lord! is imminent. Thus, trying to increase your doubt that it will not happen. In actuality, all the crazy is just part of the process to the promise. GOD's Purpose will be fulfilled before GOD's Promise!

Just stay the course --- it will result in the expected agreement of the Yes! LORD.

PRAYER:
Thank you GOD for the Yes-LORD! as I continue to build a personal relationship with you. Guide and provide for me the confidence needed as I affirm my decision to respond with faith to believe and trust your faithfulness in the process to the promise! In JESUS Name—Amen!

YES! LORD

MY NOTES:

_____
_____
_____
_____
_____
_____
_____
_____
_____
_____
_____
_____
_____
_____
_____
_____

YES! LORD

MY PRAYER:

_____
_____
_____
_____
_____
_____
_____
_____
_____
_____
_____
_____
_____

Day 19—DOER

James 1:22 (NLT) *"But don't just listen to GOD's word. You must do what it says. Otherwise, you are only fooling yourselves."*

❖ Be a doer of the word and not a hearer only

When examining the word DOER, it is someone who takes action rather than just merely talk or think. It also means to carry out or put into effect a plan, order, or course of action to get an expected result. In addition, it means someone who does something.

To be a DOER requires us to "do" something. As a DOER it will require us to stay diligent in carrying out the instructions we have been given. We must act upon the information and execute. If we find ourselves telling our own story or even making some excuse as to why we have failed to DO---know that we are being hearers only!

Be reminded, that any goals or plans that we have set to achieve to get done will require action on our part. Take the time to list the things you need to DO and get moving. Take action and be the DOER!

Just before you start to DO your own thing or list, let us not forget, by the way, that GOD also blesses those that DO His Word and Works.

So, check that list and see –What does GOD want from you or for you to do too!

PRAYER:
Thank you GOD for the ability to be a DOER! Regardless of where I am or where I am supposed to be, please do help me to hear and obey fully the instructions and word given that is needed for me to get the expected end-result that you desire for me. In JESUS Name—Amen!

DOER

MY NOTES:

_____
_____
_____
_____
_____
_____
_____
_____
_____
_____
_____
_____
_____
_____

DOER

MY PRAYER:

_____
_____
_____
_____
_____
_____
_____
_____
_____
_____
_____
_____
_____

Day 20—SEEK

Psalms 63:1-2 (KJV) *"O GOD, thou art My GOD; early will I seek thee"*

❖ Who do you seek?

When examining the word SEEK, it is to search or look for something or someone with the intent to find or discover. SEEK also means to consult. In addition, SEEK means an attempt to obtain, acquire or secure.

There are many times in our lives that we may need to SEEK to find answers to questions we have or even look for what next steps to take or make. When faced with these things, who do we seek to consult?

More than likely, we look to connect with those who we think may be the subject matter expert for what we are dealing with, and sometimes it just may be someone who we "think" may know or someone available at the time. The answers, directions, or information we receive from them may be hit or miss for what is needed. Nevertheless, as we continue to build a trusting relationship with GOD, I recommend the following:

1. SEEK GOD in everything that you do.
2. SEEK GOD concerning every aspect of your life.
3. SEEK GOD in what to say and how to pray!

As we do, we will discover that HIS counsel is *pure* and *sure*. GOD is the MASTER consultant.

SEEK GOD!

PRAYER:
Thank you LORD GOD for your word that says to SEEK you while you can be found and call upon you while you are near (Isaiah 55:6). As I seek your presence for guidance, instructions, direction, provisions, and protection, for all the many challenges I face, continue to help me to learn who GOD is and discover that you LORD GOD are well able to be and provide all things I need and always have my best interest in mind. In JESUS Name—Amen!

SEEK

MY NOTES:

_____
_____
_____
_____
_____
_____
_____
_____
_____
_____
_____
_____
_____
_____
_____
_____
_____

SEEK

MY PRAYER:

_____
_____
_____
_____
_____
_____
_____
_____
_____
_____
_____
_____
_____
_____

Day 21—ASK

James 4:2b (KJV) *"Ye have not because ye ask not."*

❖ JUST ASK...

When examining the word ASK is it to make a request. ASK also means to say something to obtain answers and information or to invite someone to join us on an outing. In addition, ASK means the price at which an item is offered for sale.

To ASK does place us in a position of transparency to show we have a need, want, or desire. For the most part, when we go to an individual to ASK, there is an unstated belief that the individual has or can get us what we need or desire.

With that said---How often do we pass up an opportunity to receive or get what we need, want, or desire because we simply fail to JUST ASK.

PRAYER:
Thank you GOD for being the Creator who can do all things exceedingly abundantly above all that we ask or think. With GOD all things are possible, and we choose to not limit you in any area of our lives. We simply ask with anticipation and expectation that GOD's perfect will be done. In JESUS Name—Amen!

ASK

MY NOTES:

_____
_____
_____
_____
_____
_____
_____
_____
_____
_____
_____
_____
_____
_____
_____

ASK

MY PRAYER:

_____
_____
_____
_____
_____
_____
_____
_____
_____
_____
_____
_____
_____
_____

Day 22—FRIEND

James 2:23 (NKJV) *"And so it happened just as the Scriptures say: Abraham believed GOD and GOD counted him as righteous because of his faith. He was called the Friend of GOD."*

❖ Who is really my FRIEND?

When examining the word FRIEND, it is a person whom one knows and has a relational bond. FRIEND also means someone who is a firm and constant supporter who cares and is loyal. In addition, FRIEND means someone who is has allegiance to another and is on the same side and not an enemy.

To be a FRIEND or to have a FRIEND is relational. Therefore, a relationship will be required to become or to have a FRIEND. This relationship must be established and built to become a FRIEND-ship. That journey in developing the FRIEND-ship will create the bonds that will be defined in moments of how many times *have you have been there* for each other.

It states in Proverbs *18:24 (KJV) "A man that hath friends must show himself friendly: and there is a friend that sticketh closer than a brother."* Know this—if we need to heal from hurts and disappointment from those we have called our FRIEND ---begin by starting to establish and build a FRIEND-ship with GOD. He is the one TRUE FRIEND!

PRAYER:
Thank you GOD for being the friend that sticks closer than a brother. GOD you never leave nor forsake me even in good or bad times. GOD you are the source of encouragement, support, and help that is always needed daily. Thank you for being my FRIEND. In JESUS Name—Amen!

FRIEND

MY NOTES:

_____
_____
_____
_____
_____
_____
_____
_____
_____
_____
_____
_____

FRIEND

MY PRAYER:

_____
_____
_____
_____
_____
_____
_____
_____
_____
_____
_____
_____

Day 23—FAITH

Luke 22:31-32 (KJV) *"And the LORD said, 'Simon, Simon! behold, Satan has desired to have you, that he may sift you as wheat. But I have prayed for thee, that thy faith fail not; and when thou art converted, strengthen thy brethren"*

❖ Have FAITH in GOD

When examining the word FAITH, it is to have a strong belief in something or someone. FAITH also means to accept as true or real. In addition, FAITH is a firmly held opinion or conviction.

FAITH is rooted in a core belief that has been either taught or accepted based on one's value and confidence in someone or something. FAITH is hope in action--the expectation and desire for something to happen.

Although when operating in FAITH there are elements of risk and vulnerability that are exposed as one awaits the possibility. Nevertheless, the strength of the core belief and expectation we have can push us pass the risk, doubt, and vulnerability to see the awaited possibility through.

It is great to know that even the LORD prayed for us that our FAITH would not fail, no matter how a situation or circumstance may appear. Draw the strength needed from knowing that to keep the FAITH.

PRAYER:
Thank you LORD GOD for the faith needed to believe you are GOD. For the word of GOD says, that faith comes by hearing, and hearing by the word of GOD. Now faith is the substance of things hoped for, the evidence of things not seen. Without FAITH it is impossible to please GOD! In JESUS Name—Amen!

FAITH

MY NOTES:

_____
_____
_____
_____
_____
_____
_____
_____
_____
_____
_____
_____
_____
_____
_____

FAITH

MY PRAYER:

_____
_____
_____
_____
_____
_____
_____
_____
_____
_____
_____
_____
_____
_____

Day 24—BELIEVE

Hebrews 11:6 (KJV) *"But without faith it is impossible to please HIM: for he that cometh to GOD must believe that HE is, and that HE is a rewarder of them that diligently seek him."*

❖ BELIEVE--ALL Things are Possible!

When examining the word BELIEVE it is to hold as an opinion; to think or suppose. BELIEVE also means to feel sure of the truth of something or someone. In addition, BELIEVE means to have certainty of one's capability of doing something.

To BELIEVE requires having a foundational element of faith. No matter how big or small one's faith is, the belief is what holds the capacity needed to stand firm. Sometimes we may have to determine we have UNBELIEF before we can increase our capacity to actually start to BELIEVE. As did a parent regarding his child in the Word of GOD *–Mark 9:23-24 (NKJV) "JESUS said to him, if you can believe, all things are possible to him who believes. Immediately the father of the child cried out and said with tears, LORD, I believe; help my unbelief!"*

PRAYER:
Thank you GOD that you are willing to help me to overcome any areas of my life that I have unbelief. Even when I may struggle to even BELIEVE you GOD, I desire to increase my capacity to BELIEVE GOD in matters that I have failed to do so. Help me in my unbelief to start the journey to BELIEVE that ALL things are possible. In JESUS Name—Amen!

BELIEVE

MY NOTES:

_____

_____

_____

_____

_____

_____

_____

_____

_____

_____

_____

_____

_____

_____

BELIEVE

MY PRAYER:

_____

_____

_____

_____

_____

_____

_____

_____

_____

_____

_____

_____

_____

Day 25—TRUST

Proverbs 3:5-7 (NKJV) *"Trust in the LORD with all your heart and lean not to your own understanding; In all your ways acknowledge HIM and HE shall direct your paths. Do not be wise in your own eyes; fear the LORD and depart from evil."*

❖ Who do you TRUST?

When examining the word TRUST, it is to rely and depend on. TRUST also means to believe in the truth, ability, and strength of. In addition, TRUST is to allow someone to have, use or look after something important or valuable; commit to the safekeeping of.

TRUST can be viewed as a virtue that take time to build up but can be shattered in a moment.

Since TRUST is fragile, one must handle TRUST with care. When TRUST is solid it can carry us *until*. TRUST can also be the deposit or down payment that will function as a barter currency in situation where we lack the actual things needed.

TRUST is very valuable, and its safekeeping is a necessity that is essential, highly recommended, and should not be overlooked or missed.

PRAYER:
Thank you LORD GOD for in you do I put my TRUST. As I choose to continue to build up my knowledge of who you are in your WORD and realize your ways and methods are not like mine, but yours will always result in the better and greater than my own. TRUSTING you become easier to do. For you are the MASTER in all that you do! In JESUS Name—Amen!

TRUST

MY NOTES:

_____
_____
_____
_____
_____
_____
_____
_____
_____
_____
_____
_____
_____
_____
_____
_____

TRUST

MY PRAYER:

_____
_____
_____
_____
_____
_____
_____
_____
_____
_____
_____
_____
_____
_____

Day 26—KNOW

Psalms 46:10a (KNJV) *"Be still and know that I am GOD!"*

❖ To KNOW or not

When examining the word KNOW it is to be very certain or sure about something or someone. KNOW also means to have developed a relationship through meeting and spending time. In addition, KNOW is to recognize or be able to distinguish one person or thing from another.

To KNOW come through learning and experiencing personally. The old adage, "TO KNOW thyself" is critical in the journey of life. Therefore, there are 3 questions that come to mind:

1. *What have you learned about yourself thus far in your life journey?*
2. *Have you taken the time needed to come to KNOW GOD in a real and personal way?*
3. If so, then ---

Do we really believe and trust GOD when HE says in *Jeremiah 29:11-12 "For I know the plans I have for you, says the LORD. They are plans for good and not for disaster, to give you a future and a hope. In those days when you pray, I will listen."*

GOD KNOWS-- but do we?

PRAYER:
Thank you GOD for being the ALL KNOWING. I pray that you help me to BE still and Know that you are GOD **and not me**. *GOD you are savior,* **and not me**; *GOD you are the true source and supply for all needs,* **and not me**. *So glad GOD you have THE PLAN,* **and not me**. *In JESUS Name—Amen*!

KNOW

MY NOTES:

_____
_____
_____
_____
_____
_____
_____
_____
_____
_____
_____
_____
_____
_____
_____

KNOW

MY PRAYER:

_____
_____
_____
_____
_____
_____
_____
_____
_____
_____
_____
_____
_____

Day 27—STRENGHT

Mark 12:30 (NKJV) *"And you shall love the LORD your GOD with all your heart, with all your souls, with all your mind, and with all your strength. This is the first commandment."*

❖ Even the strong needs some STRENGHT

When examining the word STRENGHT, it is the capacity of an object or substance to withstand great force or pressure. STRENGHT also means a good or beneficial quality or attribute of a person or thing. In addition, STRENGHT is the quality or state of being strong.

Most people have been in an interview where the question may have been asked "What are your STRENGTHS?" The response is normally a list of beneficial qualities or attributes we have deem helps us shine brighter than the next person. Nevertheless, when we discover our true STRENGHT it may be the physical, emotional, or mental qualities that are utilized while under pressure or dealing with situations or events that are distressing or difficult.

Therefore, if asked the same question "What are your STRENGHTS?" in those moments, would it really be the same list given during the interview? Perhaps, but more than likely NOT! – because during these types of moments in life, the STRENGHT one is operating in is not easily able to be described or articulated. For it is GOD.

The recommend, my friend—BE ye strong in the LORD and the power of HIS might --- is the charge to move forward in confidence knowing that we are only strong through Christ who strengths us and GOD is the foundation there of.

PRAYER:
Thank you GOD for being the STRENGHT and also giving me the STRENGHT needed to get through the ups and downs, highs and low, and the celebrations and disappointments that life brings. When weak, GOD is always the STRENGHT needed to be strong. In JESUS Name—Amen!

STRENGHT

MY NOTES:

_____
_____
_____
_____
_____
_____
_____
_____
_____
_____
_____
_____
_____
_____

STRENGHT

MY PRAYER:

_____
_____
_____
_____
_____
_____
_____
_____
_____
_____
_____
_____
_____

Day 28—PROGRESS

1 Timothy 4:15 (NKJV) "Meditate on these things; give yourself entirely to them, that your progress may be evident to all."

❖ PROGRESS is the straightway road to success

When examining the word PROGRESS, it is forward or onward movement toward a destination or goal. PROGRESS also means to advance or develop toward a better or more complex or complete condition.

As we decide to set goals we desire to achieve, it will be necessary to pause to do a check for PROGRESS. In the process of looking at what has been done thus far toward meeting & achieving the ultimate goal or destination, no matter how fast or slow, just remember to reward and give credit for every forward and onward movement that it took to move the mark even slightly.

Realistically, it is all the small steps and things we do that adds up to the bigger things needed to achieve what we set out to do. Take time to simply check for and recognize & reward PROGRESS.

PRAYER:
Thank you LORD for the efforts made on the journey to be better. It takes the movement of forward PROGRESS to get from better to best. Help me to realize that no matter how fast or slow, forward movement is the PROGRESS way to go! In JESUS Name—Amen!

PROGRESS

MY NOTES:

_____
_____
_____
_____
_____
_____
_____
_____
_____
_____
_____
_____
_____
_____
_____

PROGRESS

MY PRAYER:

_____
_____
_____
_____
_____
_____
_____
_____
_____
_____
_____
_____
_____
_____

Day 29—SUCCESS

Joshua 1:8 (ASV) *"This book of the law shall not depart out of thy mouth, but thou shall mediate thereon day and night, that thou may observe to do according to all that is written therein: for then thou shalt make thy way prosperous, and then thou shalt have good success."*

❖ How do you personally define SUCCESS?

When examining the word SUCCESS, it is the good or bad outcome of an undertaking. SUCCESS also means to attain or accomplish an aim or purpose.

The journey on the road to SUCCESS is filled with a lot of unexpected. Nevertheless, the driving point that fuels the journey is largely found in what and how we truly define SUCCESS for our own self. The guides and influences we utilize along the way will be a measure of what we have done with that which we have been given.

Nonetheless, during the journey, did the investment of thought, time, money, energy, or effort yield SUCCESS? And--At the end of the day, were you SUCCESS full? If not, maybe there could be a need to personally re-define SUCCESS.

PRAYER:
Thank You GOD for providing the direction to prosperity and good success. As I pray, do use the hunger and drive seen in my own ambition to help steer me to your word for guidance and clarity for SUCCESS. In JESUS Name—Amen!

SUCCESS

MY NOTES:

_____
_____
_____
_____
_____
_____
_____
_____
_____
_____
_____
_____
_____
_____

SUCCESS

MY PRAYER:

_____
_____
_____
_____
_____
_____
_____
_____
_____
_____
_____
_____
_____

Day 30---GIVE

2 Corinthians 9:6-8 (NKJV) *"... He who sows sparingly will also reap sparingly, and he who sows bountifully will also reap bountifully. So let each one give as he purposes in his heart, not grudgingly or of necessity; for GOD loves a cheerful giver. And GOD is able to make all grace abound toward you, that you, always having all sufficiency in all things, may have an abundance for every good work."*

❖ GIVE and it shall be given unto you

When examining the word GIVE, it is to freely transfer the possession of something to someone. GIVE also means to administer, commit, or entrust. In addition, GIVE means to freely devote, set aside or sacrifice for a purpose.

Most people were taught during childhood that is better to GIVE than receive. Personally, as a child, I desired to dive a bit deeper into that foundational childhood lesson being taught. I later discovered that in the common motion of the giving action, one has to open & release out of their hands the item possessed they want to GIVE. That open- release provides the opportunity to immediately go into a common receiving action as well. The common receiving motion by hand is to open and embrace the item given.

Basically, hands cannot receive if the hands are not open to give & hands cannot give if the hands are not open to receive. Call it overthinking, but that "ah-ha" moment for me (referred to as revelation) was pure genius from the Creator who has bestowed upon us the ability to give and receive—just like the Creator provides and supplies.

PRAYER:
Thank you GOD that you so loved that you gave to the world!!. GOD you constantly GIVE and FORGIVE. Help me to live my life as such cheerfully. In JESUS Name—Amen!

GIVE

MY NOTES:

_____
_____
_____
_____
_____
_____
_____
_____
_____
_____
_____
_____
_____
_____
_____

GIVE

MY PRAYER:

_____
_____
_____
_____
_____
_____
_____
_____
_____
_____
_____
_____
_____
_____

Day 31—THANKS

Psalms 107:1 (KJV) *"O give thanks unto the LORD, for he is good: For his mercy endureth for ever."*

❖ Have you given thanks?

When examining the word THANKS, it is an expression of gratitude. THANKS also means a readiness to show appreciation for someone or something. In addition, THANKS means to return kindness.

How easy it is to complain or express our dislike regarding something based on our perspective. A complaint can leave one's encounter or experience with a negative connotation. Just like a compliment can be a positive impact to a complaint ---Imagine what a small THANKS can impact. A simple THANKS can lift a heavy heart. THANKS can also immediately change a negative moment into a positive one.

So, ask yourself, to whom do you owe a simple THANKS?

PRAYER:
Thank you LORD that it is good to give thank. Help me to show gratitude of a THANKS before a complaint! So, I just want to say THANK you LORD for all you've done for me! In JESUS Name—Amen!

THANKS

MY NOTES:

_____
_____
_____
_____
_____
_____
_____
_____
_____
_____
_____
_____
_____
_____
_____

THANKS

MY PRAYER:

_____
_____
_____
_____
_____
_____
_____
_____
_____
_____
_____
_____
_____

DAY 32 –CONCERN

Psalms 138:8 (KJV) *"The LORD will perfect that which concerns me: Thy mercy, O LORD, endureth for ever. Forsake not the works of thine own hands."*

❖ To whom this may CONCERN

When examining the word CONCERN, it means to be of an important interest. CONCERN also means having to do with something or someone.

If you are CONCERNed, so is GOD. The LORD is faithful to fulfill HIS word and promises. *The word of GOD says*, "The LORD is not slack concerning his promises, as some men count slackness but is longsuffering to us-ward, not willing that any should perish, but that all should come to repentance." 2 Peter 3:9 (KLV)

PRAYER:
Thank you GOD for being concerned about me! As I hold fast to your word and promises, I await the blessings that are sure to come. GOD, you alone know the timing, the methods, and all the resources necessary to do exactly what you said you would do. In JESUS Name—Amen!

CONCERN

MY NOTES:

_____
_____
_____
_____
_____
_____
_____
_____
_____
_____
_____
_____
_____
_____
_____

CONCERN

MY PRAYER:

_____
_____
_____
_____
_____
_____
_____
_____
_____
_____
_____
_____
_____
_____

Day 33—EXCUSES

Luke 14:18a (GNT) *"When it was time for the feast, he sent his servant to tell his guest, 'Come, everything is ready!' But they all began, one after another, to make excuses."*

❖ No EXCUSES!

When examining the word EXCUSES, it is attempts to lessen the blame attaching to a fault or offense. EXCUSES also means to defend or justify. In addition, EXCUSES are methods of reasoning by which one tries to get release from duty or obligation.

As we continue our life's journey over a span of time, we will have opportunities to make or utilize EXCUSES to justify why something was or was not done, completed, finished etc. An EXCUSE deflects ownership of action and can be a sign of disobedience.

PRAYER:
Thank you LORD for when faced with to-do's or get-done items, you are the provider of clarity in instruction and directions as given by your Word. Help me to forge ahead in obedience with NO EXCUSES. In JESUS Name—Amen!

EXCUSES

MY NOTES:

_____
_____
_____
_____
_____
_____
_____
_____
_____
_____
_____
_____
_____
_____

EXCUSES

MY PRAYER:

_____
_____
_____
_____
_____
_____
_____
_____
_____
_____
_____
_____
_____
_____

Day 34—CHOOSE

Joshua 24:15a (KJV) *"And if it seem evil unto you to serve the LORD, choose you this day who ye will serve"*

❖ You have a choice in the matter

When examining the word CHOOSE it is an act of selecting or making a decision when faced with two or more possibilities of such a selection. It also means to pick out or select someone or something as being the best or most appropriate of two or more alternatives.
Every morning as the day begins we have the ability to CHOOSE.
Whether it is a thought, activity, or emotion, when we CHOOSE to make an intentional choice—it will set in motion consequences impacting that choice we chose.

Take a moment to just review or list what you CHOOSE this day?

PRAYER:
Thank you GOD for giving me the ability to CHOOSE. My desire is for any plans I have or things I have decided to do are to be GOD-centered and not merely self-centered. I CHOOSE ye this day! In JESUS Name— Amen!

CHOOSE

MY NOTES:

_____
_____
_____
_____
_____
_____
_____
_____
_____
_____
_____
_____
_____
_____
_____

CHOOSE

MY PRAYER:

_____
_____
_____
_____
_____
_____
_____
_____
_____
_____
_____
_____
_____

Day 35—FAITHFULNESS

Psalms 143:1 (NKJV) *"Hear my prayer, O LORD, give ear to my supplications! In your faithfulness answer me, and in your righteousness."*

❖ How great is your FAITHFULNESS?

When examining the word FAITHFULNESS, it is the quality of being trustworthy demonstrated by continual loyalty and support. FAITHFULNESS also means to remain loyal, reliable, and steadfast. In addition, FAITHFULNESS means to be able to perform consistently well and to be trusted.

If choosing a friend, companion, or mate to journey together through the good and extremely difficult times of life, one of the essential and core character traits one would desire would be FAITHFULNESS. This character trait will bring about peace in both the heart and mind that will help any type of relationship to thrive and survive all its unique challenges.

FAITHFULNESS will build trust and keeps it intact because of its consistency demonstrated in both the best and worst of times—time after time!

PRAYER:
Thank you GOD for your FAITHFULNESS! Even as I continue to learn to lean and depend on you for all things, no matter in what state I am, you can be trusted to deliver, save, and come through just as you purposed and promised accordingly to your word! GREAT is THY FAITHFULNESS! In JESUS Name—Amen!

FAITHFULNESS

MY NOTES:

_____
_____
_____
_____
_____
_____
_____
_____
_____
_____
_____
_____
_____
_____
_____
_____
_____

FAITHFULNESS

MY PRAYER:

_____
_____
_____
_____
_____
_____
_____
_____
_____
_____
_____
_____
_____
_____
_____

Day 36—WAIT

Psalms 27:14 *(NKJV) "Wait on the LORD: Be of good courage, and HE shall strengthen your heart; Wait, I say, on the LORD!"*

❖ Waiting period—we all have one

When examining the word WAIT it is to stay where one is or delay action until a particular time. WAIT also means to be left until a later time before being dealt with or handled. In addition, WAIT means to remain in readiness for some purpose-- indicating that one is eagerly impatient to do something or for something to happen.

Are you currently in a waiting period—waiting on something to come, to happen, or even waiting on a promise from GOD to manifest? See, life places us in a position to WAIT—whether we like it or not! It is amazing how none of us really like to WAIT.

Often times we tend to murmur and complain when we are required to WAIT. As we continue to develop a spiritually mature relationship with GOD, we will learn that waiting is a *necessary* part of the process to fulfill HIS purpose and to receive the promise.

Therefore, I say, welcome to the WAITING room my friend!

PRAYER:
Thank you GOD for helping me to understand there is purpose in the WAIT. Since waiting is part of the process to the promise, I pray you will help me to be of good courage, and to be cheerful while I WAIT. In JESUS Name—Amen!

WAIT

MY NOTES:

_____
_____
_____
_____
_____
_____
_____
_____
_____
_____
_____
_____
_____
_____
_____
_____
_____

WAIT

MY PRAYER:

_____
_____
_____
_____
_____
_____
_____
_____
_____
_____
_____
_____
_____
_____

Day 37—LEARN

Isaiah 1:16-17a (NKJV) *"Wash yourselves, make yourselves clean; Put away the evil of your doings from before My eyes. Cease to do evil, Learn to do good."*

❖ Learning should never end

When examining the word LEARN it is to gain or acquire knowledge or a skill in something by study, experience, observation, or being taught. LEARN also means to commit to memory.

The process of learning starts as an infant to an adult. To LEARN can be both formal or informal in the methods and tools utilized. Our brains have a high capacity to retain information as we seek to increase our knowledge and skill capacity. Nevertheless, the hunger to feed that capacity still remains a choice by the individual user.

Do you want to LEARN? If so, challenge yourself to *intentionally* LEARN something new daily. It is up to you to do!

PRAYER:
Thank you LORD for being the All-wise & All-knowing teacher. Create in me an appetite to desire to learn first of you—then all other things too! In JESUS Name—Amen!

LEARN

MY NOTES:

_____
_____
_____
_____
_____
_____
_____
_____
_____
_____
_____
_____
_____
_____
_____
_____

LEARN

MY PRAYER:

_____
_____
_____
_____
_____
_____
_____
_____
_____
_____
_____
_____
_____
_____
_____

Day 38—ABIDE

John 15:4-5 (NKJV) *"Abide in Me, and I in you. As the branch cannot bear fruit of itself, unless it abides in the vine, neither can you, unless you abide in Me. I am the vine; you are the branches. He who abides in Me, and I in him, bears much fruit; for without Me you can do nothing."*

❖ Are you connected?

When examining the word ABIDE, it means to live or dwell. ABIDE also means to act or conduct oneself in accordance to an established way, rule, decision, or recommendation. In addition, ABIDE means to remain or be present, held, or kept.

To ABIDE requires one to stay in a particular place for a while which will usually result in conforming to the surrounding environment and behaviors. A mutual connection develops and becomes one of the reasons the individual will remain there without being forced to do so. Sooner than later, the individual begins to talk like, walk like, and live like those with whom they ABIDE. The nurtured growth in the connection will produce a relationship that can either be positive or negative, refreshing or draining based upon the environment.

Therefore, we should often take a moment to inspect where or with whom we tend to ABIDE.

PRAYER:
Thank you GOD for being the vine that is life-giving. As I partake of your word daily and seek to live it out accordingly, I am living the branch-life that will produce much! For being separated and apart from you, I can do NO-THING! Abiding in you makes ALL-THINGS a possibility for doing so is a surrender unto you, your method, your ways and your precise timing. In JESUS Name—Amen!

ABIDE

MY NOTES:

_____
_____
_____
_____
_____
_____
_____
_____
_____
_____
_____
_____
_____
_____
_____
_____

ABIDE

MY PRAYER:

_____
_____
_____
_____
_____
_____
_____
_____
_____
_____
_____
_____
_____

Day 39—REST

Matthews 11:28-29 (NLT) *"Then JESUS said, 'Come to me, all of you who are weary and carry heavy burdens, and I will give you rest. Take my yoke upon you. Let me teach you, because I am humble and gentle at heart, and you will find rest for your souls."*

❖ Rest is required!

When examining the word REST, it is to cease from work or movement in order to relax, refresh, and recover strength and not to engage in strenuous or stressful activity. REST also means to place upon. In addition, REST is an interval of silence of a specific or specified duration.

Can you identify exactly where is your place of REST?

Most people have difficulty setting apart a place/time to unplug from the normality of work and responsibilities. In failing to do so we easily become weary, tired, and heavily burdened. Sometimes we must purposefully determine a place and space to REST. In doing so it allows for us to relax, refresh, recover, and encounter the very presence of GOD in that place and space.

If GOD, the Creator of the world and universe took time to REST –when will you?

PRAYER:
Thank you LORD GOD for being the ultimate example that REST is required. As I work hard and labor to achieve getting things done, help me to learn to purposefully REST knowing what still needs to be done can only be done through me trusting you through it to do it. GOD, I choose to REST for you GOT THIS! In JESUS Name—Amen!

REST

MY NOTES:

_____
_____
_____
_____
_____
_____
_____
_____
_____
_____
_____
_____
_____
_____
_____

REST

MY PRAYER:

_____
_____
_____
_____
_____
_____
_____
_____
_____
_____
_____
_____
_____
_____
_____

Day 40—PROMISES

2 Corinthians 1:20 (NKJV) *"For all the promises of GOD in HIM are Yes, and in HIM Amen, to the glory of GOD through us."*

❖ Make, Break, or Keep—who's to say?

When examining the word PROMISES, it is declarations or assurances made that one will definitely do, give, or arrange something particular to happen. PROMISES also means to pledge, undertake, or declare that a particular occurrence or situation will happen.

Most of us can think about a time when we have been impacted by PROMISES. Those given to us, those made by us, and even those that were broken.   The emotions experienced by the impact can range from being excited to being disappointed.

When we really think about the *who* is making the promises, we tend to fail to *really* realize that life situations are subject to happen that will cause us to not be able to control an outcome to fulfill the PROMISES made.

Nevertheless, but GOD who is in total control is well able to fulfill all His PROMISES made.

GOD never fails.

PRAYER:
Thank you GOD for your PROMISES. As I abide in your word, I am declaring the same --- "For when GOD made a promise.., because HE could swear by no one greater, HE swore by himself saying. 'Surely blessing I will bless you and multiplying I will multiply you.' And so, after I patiently endured, I shall also obtain the promises." In JESUS Name—Amen!

PROMISES

MY NOTES:

_____
_____
_____
_____
_____
_____
_____
_____
_____
_____
_____
_____
_____
_____

PROMISES

MY PRAYER:

_____
_____
_____
_____
_____
_____
_____
_____
_____
_____
_____
_____
_____
_____

Day 41—CHOSEN

Matthews 20:16 (NKJV) *"So the last will be first and the first last. For many are called, but few chosen."*

❖ Anointed & Appointed to carry out the plan

When examining the word CHOSEN it means having been selected as the best or most appropriate. CHOSEN also means those who are special or different typically in a way thought to be favored or unfair.

The Oral Roberts University provides a commentary that is most appropriate for CHOSEN:
"GOD chose you before the foundation of the world. GOD has a plan and an incredible destiny for you; whether you arrive there or not is entirely up to you. –Pray that GOD will give you the grace to not only understand that you have been CHOSEN but also to realize what you have been CHOSEN for. May you become more and more aware of the calling that is over your life and have the strength and capacity to fulfill it." --- Oral Roberts University

PRAYER:
Thank you GOD for choosing me even when I had not chosen you. GOD, I pray you will give me the grace to not only understand that I have been CHOSEN but also give me the clarity needed to really know what I have been CHOSEN for. My desire is to fulfill the purpose, plan, and calling on my life in its fullness. Provide me the strength and capacity to do it exceedingly abundantly above all that one could think, ask, or imagine— Be ye glorified GOD! In JESUS Name—Amen!

MY NOTES:

_____
_____
_____
_____
_____
_____
_____
_____
_____
_____
_____
_____
_____
_____
_____

MY PRAYER:

_____
_____
_____
_____
_____
_____
_____
_____
_____
_____
_____
_____
_____
_____

Day 42—GREATER

John 14:12 (NKJV) *"Most assuredly, I say to you, he who believes in Me the works that I do he will do also; and greater works than these he will do, because I go to My Father."*

❖ Nothing less but GREATER

When examining the word GREATER it is of the ability, quality, or eminence considerably above the normal or average, Greater also means larger than similar kinds; very large or imposing.

As we face overwhelming demands and challenges, we tend to look at and see all the obstacles that magnify the problem or issues. Nevertheless, if we believe in GOD, the ultimate problem-solver, and seek HIM to provide the strategy/resolution to what we face, knowing that our own trust factor in HIM has to be in full-effect, we will discover HE is the GREATER THAN. GOD the Father, Son, and Holy Spirit are unified as one to be our help in doing GREATER.

GOD is greater than any problem, person, place, thing, or situation we face. As we stay obedient to HIS word, guidance, directions, and instructions our faith and confidence should grow to be doers of HIS word & works to see the triumphant victory that shall be according to HIS will, purpose, and plan.

PRAYER:
Thank you GOD for being the GREATER in any situation. No matter who, what, when, or where I face challenges and demands that will require me to believe you for the outcome, GOD as creator you are GREATER! In JESUS Name—Amen!

GREATER

MY NOTES:

_____
_____
_____
_____
_____
_____
_____
_____
_____
_____
_____
_____
_____
_____
_____
_____

GREATER

MY PRAYER:

_____
_____
_____
_____
_____
_____
_____
_____
_____
_____
_____
_____
_____
_____

Day 43—WALK

Colossians 1:9-10 (NKJV) *"For this reason we also, since the day we heard it, do not cease to pray for you, and to ask that you may be filled with the knowledge of HIS will in all wisdom and spiritual understanding; that you may walk worthy of the LORD, fully pleasing HIM, being fruitful in every good work and increasing in the knowledge of GOD."*

❖ Walk into your blessings!

When examining the word WALK it is to move at a regular pace by lifting and setting down each foot in turn. WALK also means to guide, accompany, or escort as an act of traveling on foot. In addition, WALK can mean a lifestyle or living example.

Have you ever heard the idiom "Walk the Walk"? It is normally said or used to infer that one is to do the things that one says one will do.

With that said, ask yourself --- Are you currently walking the WALK worthy of the call on your life? If not, why not?

PRAYER:
Thank you LORD for the purpose and plans you have for my life. Help me walk worthy of the call upon my life to fully please you. Be Glorified in all that is done as I walk it out. In JESUS Name—Amen!

WALK

MY NOTES:

_____
_____
_____
_____
_____
_____
_____
_____
_____
_____
_____
_____
_____
_____

WALK

MY PRAYER:

_____
_____
_____
_____
_____
_____
_____
_____
_____
_____
_____
_____
_____
_____

Day 44—TALK

3 John 1:13-14 (NIV) *"I have much to write you, but I do not want to do so with pen and ink. I hope to see you soon, and we will talk face-to-face."*

❖ Need some TALK therapy?

When examining the word TALK it is to speak in order to give information or express ideas or feelings. TALK also means to communicate by spoken words, conversation, or discussion. In addition, TALK is the power of speech.

An area one has complete control over is the mouth. How we choose to TALK to one another and what we choose to TALK about a controllable. We have the need to talk to express our thoughts, ideas, and feelings.

Just remember, our TALK can have a significant impact to outcomes in our lives.

PRAYER:
Thank you LORD for prayer. Prayer is a form of TALK therapy that allows me to have intimate conversations with you about any and everything that is happening in my life. I am grateful that our TALK has the power to change me, and those things that concern me because you are the All-Powerful and ALMIGHTY GOD. Our TALK also allows me to receive instructions, guidance and direction as needed and when needed. With that said, Let's TALK often! In JESUS Name—Amen!

TALK

MY NOTES:

TALK

MY PRAYER:

Day 45—COMMUNION

2 Corinthians 6:14 (ASV) *"The grace of the LORD Jesus Christ, and the love of GOD, and the communion of the Holy Spirit, be with you all."*

❖ Spiritual intimacy

When examining the word COMMUNION, it is the sharing or exchange of intimate thoughts and feelings often on a mental or spiritual level. COMMUNION also means the service of Christian worship at which bread and wine are consecrated and shared. In addition, COMMUNION is fellowship and close rapport with someone or others.

COMMUNION is an investment of shared time and space with another person. It can often be referred to as "breaking bread" with someone which denotes more than just eating. It is a shared sense of brotherhood or sisterhood with a significant connection because bread is such a life-giving source of nourishment. In Christian worship, COMMUNION is an act of remembering Christ. Never forgetting the sacrificial love shown.

All in all, COMMUNION is a significant meaningful connection. Do you have one?

PRAYER:
Thank you GOD for the need to have COMMUNION with you. As we break bread and drink of the fruit of the vine, I do so in remembrance of all the sacrificial love shown through Christ. I pray I receive healing and wholeness now and forevermore. In JESUS Name—Amen!

COMMUNION

MY NOTES:

_____
_____
_____
_____
_____
_____
_____
_____
_____
_____
_____
_____
_____
_____

COMMUNION

MY PRAYER:

_____
_____
_____
_____
_____
_____
_____
_____
_____
_____
_____
_____
_____

Day 46---HOLY

1 Peter 1:15-16 (ASV) *"But like as he who called you is holy, be ye yourselves also holy in all manner of living; because it is written, Ye shall be holy; for I am holy."*

❖ Holy, Holy, Holy

When examining the word HOLY, it means totally devoted or dedicated to GOD. HOLY also means sacred or consecrated to GOD.

The three-fold Holy, Holy, Holy is an expression to emphasize the Holiness of GOD. As stated in **Isaiah 6:3 (KJV)** *"And one cried unto another, and said, Holy, Holy, Holy is the LORD of hosts: the whole earth is full of his glory."* Holiness of GOD is morally perfect, pure, and set apart from all sin. To rediscover GOD and HIS Holiness this can be done by embarking upon a Bible Study regimen to learn about GOD. As we study we will begin to recognize the extent of GOD's Love, Grace, and Forgiveness and how powerful GOD truly is. We can only become more like HIM through learning more about HIM.

PRAYER:
Thank you LORD GOD that you are far above us all in your majestic splendor and is HOLY, HOLY, HOLY. As I seek to live HOLY and be set apart for your special use, keep me aware and away from the common profane things of daily living. Consecrated, and sacred, I pray. In JESUS Name—Amen!

HOLY

MY NOTES:

_____
_____
_____
_____
_____
_____
_____
_____
_____
_____
_____
_____
_____
_____

HOLY

MY PRAYER:

_____
_____
_____
_____
_____
_____
_____
_____
_____
_____
_____
_____
_____
_____

Day 47—HUMBLE

1 Peter 5:6 (KJV) *"Humble yourselves therefore under the mighty power of GOD, that he may exalt you in due time."*

❖ Check your vital signs

When examining the word HUMBLE it means of modest pretensions or dimensions.   HUMBLE also means having or showing a low estimate or view of one's own importance. In addition, HUMBLE is being lower in dignity or importance.

As I reflect upon some HUMBLE times in my own life, I would describe HUMBLE as this: For one to show humility or to HUMBLE themselves, it requires having a *quiet* confidence in knowing who you are and recognizing (self-awareness) that it is *not necessary* to try to convince others of who you are nor what you know. In addition, as I continue to reflect on my own experience, being HUMBLE also is having the ability to admit deficiencies and struggles but also (at the same time) having the willingness to get and receive the assistance, aide, or help needed.

PRAYER:
Thank you LORD for the true humility that empowers us to rise up in strength to do all the things GOD has purposed and called us to do! As I strive to be HUMBLE in all endeavors, help me to continue to learn that my worth and value—of who I am, what I know, and what I can do, --all comes from you! In JESUS Name—Amen!

HUMBLE

MY NOTES:

_____
_____
_____
_____
_____
_____
_____
_____
_____
_____
_____
_____
_____
_____
_____
_____
_____

HUMBLE

MY PRAYER:

_____
_____
_____
_____
_____
_____
_____
_____
_____
_____
_____
_____
_____
_____
_____

Day 48—MIRACLES

John 12:37 (KJV) *"But though he had done so many miracles before them, yet they believed not on him."*

❖ Do you believe in MIRACLES?

When examining the word MIRACLES, these are highly improbable or extraordinary events, developments, or accomplishments that appear to be contrary to the laws of nature and is regarded as an act of GOD. MIRACLES are also something admired as a marvelous creation or example of a particular type of science, skill, event, or action that is considered amazing, extraordinary, or unexpected. In addition, MIRACLES are the work of the divine GOD, a wonder, marvel, sensation that is an unexplainable occurrence.

If one desires to see or receive a MIRACLE, one must be in a MIRACLE category. Your situation or circumstances that you face will get to a point that all remaining options are no longer options and things looks pretty bleak in happening or getting resolved. Subsequently, a glimpse of hope that is fueled by faith to believe is what will ignite the elements required for a MIRACLE.

Focus to BELIEVE GOD! For it is GOD who has the power & provisions to produce the improbable!

PRAYER:
Thank you LORD for being the MIRACLE-working GOD! Whether we call MIRACLES the supernatural or an unexplainable occurrence, nonetheless, with GOD's assistance, intervention, or even simply GOD's purpose or plan things can & will happen! Is there anything to hard or impossible for GOD—my answer is 'NO" if I just have faith to believe GOD and expect the MIRACLE! I believe GOD! In JESUS Name—Amen!

MIRACLES

MY NOTES:

_____
_____
_____
_____
_____
_____
_____
_____
_____
_____
_____
_____
_____
_____
_____

MIRACLES

MY PRAYER:

_____
_____
_____
_____
_____
_____
_____
_____
_____
_____
_____
_____
_____
_____

Day 49—COME

Matthews 14:27-29a (NKJV) *"But immediately JESUS spoke to them, saying, 'Be of good cheer! It is I; do not be afraid.' And Peter answered HIM and said, 'LORD, if it is you, command me to come to you on the water.' So, HE said, COME."*

❖ It's an invitation ---How will you respond?

When examining the word COME it is to move or travel toward or into a place thought of as near or familiar to join someone in participating in a specified activity or course of action. COME also means to occur, happen, experience, or take place. In addition, COME means to reach eventually a certain condition or state of mind.

Will you come? Is a question that may be presented as an invitation.

When asked, does one have to ponder whether she or he will or not? As you reflect, consider why?

PRAYER:
Thank you GOD that you desire me to COME unto you to worship, pray, and praise! The invitation to COME actually does leave the choice up to me to accept. I come. In JESUS Name—Amen!

COME

MY NOTES:

_____
_____
_____
_____
_____
_____
_____
_____
_____
_____
_____
_____
_____
_____
_____

COME

MY PRAYER:

_____
_____
_____
_____
_____
_____
_____
_____
_____
_____
_____
_____
_____
_____

Day 50—OBEDIENCE

Romans 16:19 (NIV) *"Everyone has heard about your obedience, so I rejoice because of you; but I want you to be wise about what is good, and innocent about what is evil."*

❖ To obey is better than sacrifice

When examining the word OBEDIENCE, it means in accordance with; OBEDIENCE also means compliance with an order, request, law, or submission to another's authority. In addition, OBEDIENCE means willingly being submissive to another's will.

How importance is OBEDIENCE in the word of GOD? There are many scriptures that one could use to discover the answer. Here are a few that come to mind:

1. *Deuteronomy 11:1* (GW) "Love the LORD your GOD and do what he wants you to do. Always obey his laws, rules, and commands.
2. *Deuteronomy 11:26-28* (KJV) "Behold. I set before you this day a blessing and a curse, a blessing, if ye obey the commandments of the LORD your GOD, which I command you this day: and a cure, if ye will not obey the commandments of the LORD your GOD.
3. *Romans 6:16b-*(GW) "..Either your master is sin or your master is OBEDIENCE. Letting sin be your master leads to death. Letting OBEDIENCE be your master leads to GOD's approval."

To obey is better than sacrifice! My own personal truth discovery is because OBEDIENCE is the *ultimate* self-sacrifice.

PRAYER:
Thank you GOD that OBEDIENCE matters and is a way to show our love back to you. As I continue to build my personal relationship with you and continue learning about you and trusting in you more and more OBEDIENCE to your will, word, and way just become a lifestyle. My steps are ordered by you LORD GOD. In JESUS Name—Amen!

OBEDIENCE

MY NOTES:

_____
_____
_____
_____
_____
_____
_____
_____
_____
_____
_____
_____
_____
_____
_____

OBEDIENCE

MY PRAYER:

_____
_____
_____
_____
_____
_____
_____
_____
_____
_____
_____
_____
_____
_____

Day 51—TRANSPARENCY

Psalms 51:6 (ASV) *"Behold, thou desirest truth in the inward parts; and in the hidden part thou wilt make me to know wisdom. Purify me with hyssop, and I shall be clean: Wash me, and I shall be whiter than snow."*

❖ See into me

When examining the word TRANSPARENCY, it is the quality of allowing light to pass through so that objects can be distinctly seen. TRANSPARENCY also means having thoughts, feelings, or motives that are easily perceived, detected, or seen. In addition, TRANSPARENCY means openness that is subject to public scrutiny.

There are people who struggle with areas of inefficiencies or deficiencies that have a tendency to avoid being TRANSPARENT. Many time this avoidance of TRANSPARENCY can be due to past scrutiny one has experienced or critical criticism, shame, or even embarrassment. These observations or examinations of themselves or by others has affected the desire to be honest and allow TRANSPARENCY.

Nonetheless, if we consciously and intentionally make efforts to create environments that allow people to be themselves without scrutiny, it is amazing to think and imagine what could be accomplished and achieved through TRANSPARENCY!

PRAYER:
Thank you LORD for your light that so shine in and through me. TRANSPARENCY is my desire state to be with you LORD GOD so that I can become all you created me to be without my own scrutiny. GOD you love me completely even with all my tendencies. In JESUS Name—Amen!

TRANSPARENCY

MY NOTES:

_____
_____
_____
_____
_____
_____
_____
_____
_____
_____
_____
_____
_____
_____
_____
_____

TRANSPARENCY

MY PRAYER:

_____
_____
_____
_____
_____
_____
_____
_____
_____
_____
_____
_____
_____
_____

Day 52—ISSUES

Proverbs 4:23 (NKJV) *"Keep thy heart with all diligence; For out of it springs the issues of life."*

❖ We all have them—What's yours?

When examining the word ISSUES, these are important topics or problems for debate or discussion. ISSUES also means to disagree with or challenge. In addition, ISSUES means to come, go, or flow out from.

It is important for individuals to have a safe *place* and safe *space* to vent their ISSUES without judgment. ISSUES in our lives will overflow to a point where venting will be necessary. Counseling, Therapy, and Ministry are all methods that can be utilized to help individuals "unpack" these areas of life for healthy living. Find a qualified person you can trust that can be the listening ear needed to vent the ISSUES required.

PRAYER:
Thank you GOD for being my source for help is dealing with ISSUES I have. Continue to help me to have sensitivities to any emotional needs or damages that ISSUES can cause to others. I desire to understand as much about myself and my own ISSUES that you GOD are willing to reveal to me. Your divine Healing and Resolves to ISSUES come through receiving revelation and having my own desire to become better. I want to be better GOD! In JESUS Name—Amen!

MY NOTES:

_____
_____
_____
_____
_____
_____
_____
_____
_____
_____
_____
_____
_____
_____
_____

MY PRAYER:

_____
_____
_____
_____
_____
_____
_____
_____
_____
_____
_____
_____
_____
_____
_____

Day 53—GRACE

Ephesians 2:8 (NLT) *"GOD saved you by his grace when you believed. And you can't take credit for this; it is a gift from GOD."*

❖ What is *SO* Amazing about GRACE?

When examining the word GRACE, the definition that is befitting is from a message taught by Bishop Clarence E. McClendon—that GRACE is the unmerited, unearned, and undeserved, never-failing love, favor, and enabling (miracle working) power of GOD.

GRACE is so amazing because it is always abounding. It is an outpouring of GOD himself! GRACE is the Spirit of GOD reaching out to you, available for you, in order to help you! This help is freely offered, and freely given by GOD!

Now that is amazing!

PRAYER:
Thank you GOD for your amazing GRACE! GOD, your manifold GRACE is filled with such wonder that it causes astonishment as well as gratitude and admiration. For it is GOD's GRACE that saves me, delivers me, cleanse me, and changes me. In JESUS Name—Amen!

GRACE

MY NOTES:

_____
_____
_____
_____
_____
_____
_____
_____
_____
_____
_____
_____
_____
_____
_____
_____
_____
_____

GRACE

MY PRAYER:

_____
_____
_____
_____
_____
_____
_____
_____
_____
_____
_____
_____
_____
_____
_____
_____

Day 54—VOICE ACTIVATED

Proverbs 18:21 (KJV) *"Death and Life are in the power of the tongue: And they that love it shall eat the fruit thereof."*

❖ Speak forth those things that are not as though they already are

When examining the word phrase VOICE ACTIVATED, it means to make something come to be, work, or become operative by sound produced from a person's larynx and uttered through the mouth as speech or song.

It is fascinating to study the bible and discover that the Heavens and Earth was VOICE ACTIVATED. Simply put, GOD spoke it and it was so! Also recognizing that man and woman was created in GOD's image, GOD has given believers the ability to do the same. There are many illustrations of this in the bible. A noteworthy example is the story of Ezekiel in *The Valley of the Dried Bones* (Ezekiel 37:1-14). Speak to VOICE ACTIVATE.

PRAYER:
Thank you LORD that you are GOD who is the creator and designer of all creation. The voice of the LORD is powerful; the voice of the LORD is full of majesty; I pray oh LORD that you hear my voice and let thine ear be attentive to the VOICE ACTIVATION in my supplications. For your glory and greater glory. In JESUS Name—Amen!

VOICE ACTIVATED

MY NOTES:

_____
_____
_____
_____
_____
_____
_____
_____
_____
_____
_____
_____
_____
_____
_____
_____

VOICE ACTIVATED

MY PRAYER:

_____
_____
_____
_____
_____
_____
_____
_____
_____
_____
_____
_____
_____
_____
_____

Day 55—POWER

Ephesians 1:19-21 (NLT) *"I also pray that you will understand the incredible greatness of GOD's power for us who believe him. This is the same mighty power that raised CHRIST from the dead and seated him in the place of honor at GOD's right hand in the heavenly realms. Now he is far above any ruler or authority or power or leader or anything else—not only in this world but also in the world to come."*

❖ Are you POWER packing?

When examining the word POWER, it is strength, energy, and/or a force exerted by something or someone. POWER also means a right or authority that is given or delegated to a person or body. In addition, POWER is also the ability to command, rule, influence, or control.

The POWER of GOD can transform any person's life, situation, and circumstance. Therefore, the need to tap into accessing a daily flow of POWER from GOD is a vital element to function victoriously in our life. There are a few steps that can be taken to access the daily flow of POWER. Salvation is an initial step. We confess with our mouth and believe in our heart (*Romans 10:9-10*), then abiding in the WORD of GOD and next, receive the indwelling of the Holy Spirit of GOD, to work *in us, on us, with us,* and *for us*. These are some very important key steps to do in that process to access a daily flow of POWER from GOD.

Are you a carrier of the presence and power of GOD? For it is only GOD who can empower to activate His POWER.

PRAYER:
Thank you GOD for your wonder working POWER that is always at work. GOD, you are the ultimate superhero that has ALL POWER to change anything and anyone, at any time. Continue to empower me and transform my life as you have purposed, planned, and promised. In JESUS Name—Amen!

MY NOTES:

_____
_____
_____
_____
_____
_____
_____
_____
_____
_____
_____
_____
_____
_____

POWER

MY PRAYER:

_____
_____
_____
_____
_____
_____
_____
_____
_____
_____
_____
_____
_____

Day 56—MAKE ME

Psalms 23: 1-3 (ESV) *"The LORD is my shepherd; I shall not want. He makes me lie down in green pastures. He leads me beside still waters. He restores my soul. He leads me in paths of righteousness for his name's sake."*

❖ Are you looking for a challenge?

When examining the word phase MAKE ME it means to compel someone to do something. MAKE ME also means cause someone to become or exist or bring about. In addition, MAKE ME mean to form, create, or alter something into something else.

During my childhood, I can recall when the word MAKE ME was used most often—It was usually an older, and bigger relative, friend, or foe that approached me to "dare" me to do something that would more than likely lead to getting in trouble or disciplined. As small in stature as I was and scared at that time, I would say—You can't MAKE ME do that!

That was a pretty bold statement from the little in stature—person I was, responding back that way to a bigger individual that probably really could MAKE ME, if they forced me. Now as an adult, MAKE ME is no longer is that defensive challenge I saw it to be then, I now see it as an opportunity and choice I have and can decide to do, if I desire to *willingly* submit.

PRAYER:
Thank you GOD for being LORD of my life! As the Almighty GOD, the creator, you have the power to MAKE ME do, be, see, and become. I willingly submit my life to you! In JESUS Name—Amen!

MAKE ME

MY NOTES:

_____
_____
_____
_____
_____
_____
_____
_____
_____
_____
_____
_____
_____
_____
_____

MAKE ME

MY PRAYER:

_____
_____
_____
_____
_____
_____
_____
_____
_____
_____
_____
_____
_____

Day 57—REVIVE

Psalms 119:25 (NLT) *"I lie in the dust; revive me by your word."*

❖ Remove or REVIVE—You decide!

When examining the word REVIVE it means to bring back to life, energy, or strength. REVIVE also means to regain interest in or the popularity of. In addition, REVIVE mean to restore or improve the position and condition of.

The giver of life is the true source to REVIVE life. Revival comes from GOD. For when GOD speaks, REVIVAL comes forth.

Take a look at different areas of your life on today and see what needs to be REVIVED. Begin with considering some of the following:

1. Any relationships - (family, friends, networks, etc...)
2. Any dreams & career aspirations - (degrees, certifications, technology skills, a business, etc...)
3. Any health habits - (saving money, exercising, eating rights, etc....)

Also, while looking at these things ----Let us *remember* that some things may need to be ***removed*** and not REVIVED.

PRAYER:
Thank you GOD for being my source & supplier for revival. Help me to see and believe for revival. I pray GOD restores the areas in my life that need to be REVIVED and help me to part ways and release anything that needs to be removed. GOD, I pray---REVIVE me again! In JESUS Name—Amen!

MY NOTES:

_____
_____
_____
_____
_____
_____
_____
_____
_____
_____
_____
_____
_____
_____
_____

MY PRAYER:

_____
_____
_____
_____
_____
_____
_____
_____
_____
_____
_____
_____
_____
_____

Day 58—REFRESH

Jeremiah 31:25 (NIV) *"I will refresh the weary and satisfy the faint."*

❖ Oh, so satisfying!

When examining the word REFRESH it is to start over without losing the original form or information. REFRESH also means a clean slate. In addition, REFRESH means to awake, stimulate, or energize.

After having a full day of work, events, and activities, one may feel exhausted. To REFRESH yourself may typically entail a shower, rest, and some food. We should understand that it is a necessity to REFRESH spiritually, physically, mentally, and emotionally to be effective in the things we set out to do.

How one chooses to REFRESH should help to rejuvenate and stimulate the mind, body, and spirit so that executing and performing at our best can be the outcome.

PRAYER:
Thank you LORD for the times of REFRESHing that comes from your presence. When I am exhausted, tired, and/or weary REFRESH me so that I can fulfill that which I need and desire, to do. In JESUS Name— Amen!

REFRESH

MY NOTES:

_____
_____
_____
_____
_____
_____
_____
_____
_____
_____
_____
_____
_____
_____
_____

REFRESH

MY PRAYER:

_____
_____
_____
_____
_____
_____
_____
_____
_____
_____
_____
_____
_____
_____

Day 59—RENEW

Romans 12:2 (NKJV) *"And do not be conformed to this world, but be transformed by the renewing of your mind, that you may prove what is that good and acceptable and perfect will of GOD."*

❖ Think about it... You do have a right to change your mind

When examining the word RENEW it means to repair, mend, or make like new again. RENEW also means to begin again or give fresh life or strength to. In addition, RENEW means to renovate or restore something that is broken or worn out.

There was a time that after a natural disaster that impacted my home, I had the opportunity to make some extensive changes to it. Although the framework was in place, there were extensive changes made inside that one would not be able to see just looking from the outside. The same can be so when we allow the Spirit of GOD to do the same with our minds.

Although mental health and well-being is an aspect of life that has become an important focus in our present day after our entire nation experienced a pandemic. The awesome reality that mental health has always been a part of GOD's will and original plan. It is important to have a sound mind, therefore do take care of your mind as you would any other vital organ.

PRAYER:
Thank you LORD revealing things by the Spirit of GOD. As a Believer, I pray your WORD we have received not the spirit of the world, but the spirit which is of GOD that we might know the things that are freely given to us of GOD because they are spiritually discerned. The natural man or woman does not receive the things of the Spirit of GOD, for they are foolish to them; nor can they know them because those things are spiritually discerned. But as Believers we have the mind of Christ so that GOD can instruct and direct us.. As we RENEW our minds, help us to always align to know and understand your will, purpose, and plans for our lives. In JESUS Name—Amen!

RENEW

MY NOTES:

_____
_____
_____
_____
_____
_____
_____
_____
_____
_____
_____
_____
_____
_____
_____

RENEW

MY PRAYER:

_____
_____
_____
_____
_____
_____
_____
_____
_____
_____
_____
_____
_____
_____

Day 60—UPLIFT

John 12:32 (NIV) *Jesus said.." And I, if I be lifted up from the earth, I will draw all unto me."*

❖ Lift up to Uplift

When examining the word UPLIFT it is to make a person feel more cheerful, positive, or optimistic. UPLIFT also means to increase, hoist, or raise the level of. In addition, UPLIFT means to provide support to and improve.

To UPLIFT can be those efforts made to encourage and build back some hope and confidence in individuals who somehow have become discouraged, deflated, or feel defeated. People tend to hang their heads down when experiencing these types of negative emotions. Let us help to UPLIFT those who need it, especially when we see it.

PRAYER:
Thank you LORD for being the lifter of my head. As I lift up my eyes to GOD from where my strength comes, help me to also UPLIFT others in the process. As I magnify and praise your great excellency—Be Ye Lifted Up! In JESUS Name—Amen!

MY NOTES:

_____
_____
_____
_____
_____
_____
_____
_____
_____
_____
_____
_____
_____
_____
_____
_____

MY PRAYER:

_____
_____
_____
_____
_____
_____
_____
_____
_____
_____
_____
_____
_____
_____
_____

Day 61—JOY

John 15:11 (KJV) *"These things have I spoken unto you, that my joy might remain in you, and that your joy might be full."*

❖ Count it all JOY

When examining the word JOY is it a feeling of great pleasure and happiness. JOY also means gladness and delight. In addition, JOY means to rejoice.

The teachings by authors Billy Graham and Max Anders on the topic of the Holy Spirit has commentary that is most appropriate regarding JOY:

"JOY is one of the nine character qualities that are known as the Fruit of the Spirit that GOD possesses, and the Holy Spirit imparts to us and develops within us, as we live and abide in a trusting and obedient relationship with GOD. JOY is a deep sense of wellbeing that is not dependent upon favorable circumstances but is rooted in a fundamental acceptance of the confidence in the will of GOD."

JOY does not come by pursuing JOY, it is a by-product of pursing GOD.

PRAYER:
Thank you LORD GOD for in thy presence is fulness of JOY! Help me to always have a proper perspective and outlook on life for in my daily living, it is not the pursuit of happiness but the pursuit of GOD. In JESUS Name—Amen!

JOY

MY NOTES:

_____
_____
_____
_____
_____
_____
_____
_____
_____
_____
_____
_____
_____
_____
_____

JOY

MY PRAYER:

_____
_____
_____
_____
_____
_____
_____
_____
_____
_____
_____
_____
_____
_____

Day 62—PEACE

Isaiah 26:3-4 (KJV) *"Thou wilt keep him in perfect peace, whose mind is stayed on thee: because he trusteth in thee. Trust ye in the LORD for ever: for in the LORD JEHOVAH is everlasting strength."*

❖ Are you at PEACE?

When examining the word PEACE it is a state or period in which there is no war or battle. PEACE also means freedom from disturbance or tranquility. In addition, PEACE mean calm, quiet, and restful.

PEACE is another one of the nine character qualities that are known as the Fruit of the Spirit that GOD possesses, and the Holy Spirit imparts to us and develops within us as we live and abide in a trusting and obedient relationship with GOD.

PEACE is rooted in trust. If one does not have trust in a person, situation, or circumstance then PEACE will be lacking. Therefore, if we put our trust in GOD instead of things or people then we can look to understand PEACE to be –not an elimination of trouble or difficult circumstances, but as an assurance in GOD despite our circumstances!

Seek PEACE and pursuit it! If it be possible, as much as lieth in you, do all you can to live in PEACE with everyone.

PRAYER:
Thank you GOD that your PEACE is not like that of the world. The PEACE of GOD which is beyond all understand shall keep my heart and mind through Christ. In JESUS Name—Amen!

PEACE

MY NOTES:

_____
_____
_____
_____
_____
_____
_____
_____
_____
_____
_____
_____
_____
_____

PEACE

MY PRAYER:

_____
_____
_____
_____
_____
_____
_____
_____
_____
_____
_____
_____
_____

Day 63—KINDNESS

Psalms 117:2 (KJV) *"For his merciful kindness is great toward us: And the truth of the LORD endureth for ever."*

❖ Show some KINDNESS today!

When examining the word KINDNESS it is the quality of being friendly, generous, and considerate. KINDNESS also means benevolence, thoughtfulness, and compassion.

KINDNESS is another one of the nine character qualities that are known as the Fruit of the Spirit that GOD possesses, and the Holy Spirit imparts to us and develops within us as we live and abide in a trusting and obedient relationship with GOD.

KINDNESS goes beyond being "nice." KINDNESS is real love in action. KINDNESS is not an emotion or a feeling, but action drawn from the disposition of the heart. We all have a choice of whether we do something or not and be or not be—KIND. Thus, the challenge for us is to find ways, with no pre-qualifiers, motives, no conditions, and not just be KIND to your own kind, but to be KIND to *whomever* for *whatever* reason the opportunity presents itself.

PRAYER:
Thank you LORD for your mercy and everlasting KINDNESS. I pray my words, thoughts, and action be filled with KINDNESS. In JESUS Name—Amen!

KINDNESS

MY NOTES:

_____
_____
_____
_____
_____
_____
_____
_____
_____
_____
_____
_____
_____
_____
_____

KINDNESS

MY PRAYER:

_____
_____
_____
_____
_____
_____
_____
_____
_____
_____
_____
_____
_____
_____
_____

Day 64—FORGIVE

Ephesians 4:31-32 (NIV) *"Get rid of all bitterness, rage, anger, harsh words, and slander, as well as all types of evil behavior!" Instead, be kind to each other, tenderhearted, forgiving one another just as GOD through CHRIST has forgiven you."*

❖ FORGIVE and you shall be FORGIVEN

When examining the word FORGIVE it means to stop feeling angry or resentful toward someone for an offense. FORGIVE also means to exonerate. In addition, FORGIVE mean to cancel or excuse.

Hurtful attitudes and actions of others can cause us to experience ill-will feelings. These feelings then begin to harbor in our hearts and mind which can cause us to be unforgiving. Unforgiveness toward another person is toxic and can cause an infection to spread to other areas of our life. If we fail to deal with the areas and FORGIVE, the unforgiveness it can negatively escalate into anger, hatred, and even vengeance!

Remember that Vengeance is the LORD and HE is able to repay better than we can ever imagine. So, let GOD heal you and deal with those you choose to FORGIVE!

PRAYER:
Thank you LORD for being faithful and just to FORGIVE and clean me from all unrighteousness. As I confess my sins and wrong doings to you daily and receive your FORGIVEness, help me to easily FORGIVE those who hurt and disappoint me without having any resentment, anger, or regret. In JESUS Names—Amen!

FORGIVE

MY NOTES:

_____
_____
_____
_____
_____
_____
_____
_____
_____
_____
_____
_____
_____
_____
_____
_____

FORGIVE

MY PRAYER:

_____
_____
_____
_____
_____
_____
_____
_____
_____
_____
_____
_____
_____
_____

Day 65—PROTECTION

Psalm 5:11-12 (NLT) *"But let all who take refuge in you rejoice; let them sing joyful praises forever. Spread your protection over them, that all who love your name may be filled with joy. For you bless the godly, O LORD; you surround them with your shield of love."*

❖ Are you fully protected?

When examining the word PROTECTION, it is to keep safe from harm, danger, damage, or injury. PROTECTION also means to preserve, safeguard or shield; In addition, PROTECTION means to prevent something undesirable.

Many of us have some type of insurance that we expect to provide us with the PROTECTION needed in case of an accident or an emergency. In these crisis situations we hope to be fully covered from any kind of hurt, harm, damage, or danger. If there is a gap in coverage, we can discover we lack the PROTECTION we assumed we had, which can cost us greatly.

GOD provides insurance coverage that has no gaps. GOD never leave, nor forsakes and is omnipresent to always PROTECT.

Who is currently providing your coverage? Take the time to get assurance regarding your insurance needed to ensure your coverage is well worth the investment.

PRAYER:
Thank you GOD for the hedge of protection that surrounds me by your mere presence in my life. Continue to protect my going out and coming in including my property and possessions now and forevermore. In JESUS Name—Amen!

PROTECTION

MY NOTES:

_____
_____
_____
_____
_____
_____
_____
_____
_____
_____
_____
_____
_____
_____
_____

PROTECTION

MY PRAYER:

_____
_____
_____
_____
_____
_____
_____
_____
_____
_____
_____
_____
_____
_____
_____

Day 66—REJECTION

Psalms 94:14 (NIV) *"For the LORD will not reject his people; he will never forsake his inheritance."*

❖ Accepted or Rejected---You have what it takes!

When examining the word REJECTION, it is to dismiss or discard as inadequate or inappropriate. REJECTION also means to fail to show affection or concern for. In addition, REJECTION means unwanted, or failing to satisfy one's taste or preference.

Being REJECTed may be one of the most painful and difficult afflictions one experiences. Especially when REJECTION comes from a person the individual loved or admired and did not despise. REJECTION can bring about feelings of loneliness, and even the feeling of not being adequate enough. As individuals, we must come to understand that REJECTION happens to everyone. At some point in our lives, we will not be accepted, nor get what we want, nor be what someone else wants. Thus, how we decide to *respond* to REJECTION is what matters.

Seek GOD and allow GOD to heal the hurt that being REJECTed brings. GOD can heal and begin to build the self-confidence and self-esteem that may be needed. During the process, GOD can also reveal whether that REJECTION was actually a form of Projection!

Seek GOD Today!

PRAYER:
Thank you GOD for being loving and accepting of me! Help me experience your love in ways that causes me to love myself and know my worth in you. So, when REJECTION comes, it does not cause me to devalue myself in any way. For I am worthy just because I have been created to be all that GOD has deemed me to be. In JESUS Name— Amen!

REJECTION

MY NOTES:

_____
_____
_____
_____
_____
_____
_____
_____
_____
_____
_____
_____
_____
_____
_____
_____

REJECTION

MY PRAYER:

_____
_____
_____
_____
_____
_____
_____
_____
_____
_____
_____
_____
_____
_____
_____

Day 67—FORWARD

Exodus 14:15 (NKJV) *"And the LORD said to Moses, Why do you cry to me? Tell the children of Israel to go forward."*

❖ Keep Going

When examining the word FORWARD it means moving or tending onward as to make progress. FORWARD also mean in the direction that one is facing or traveling. In addition, FORWARD means toward the future; ahead of time.

There are seasons in our lives when we are stuck being preoccupied with the past and fail to focus on the future. When we position ourselves to *face* FORWARD, we can then begin to *move* FORWARD.

Let's forget those things that are behind and move FORWARD to the *New & Next.*

PRAYER:
Thank you LORD for already knowing the plan you have for me. GOD, your plan has prosperity, hope, and a future. Keep me moving FORWARD to leave things of the past, in the past. Although I may not currently be able to fully see what is up ahead, my desire is to always keep moving FORWARD into my NEW and NEXT things you have deemed for me. In JESUS Name—Amen!

FORWARD

MY NOTES:

_____
_____
_____
_____
_____
_____
_____
_____
_____
_____
_____
_____
_____
_____
_____

FORWARD

MY PRAYER:

_____
_____
_____
_____
_____
_____
_____
_____
_____
_____
_____
_____
_____
_____
_____

Day 68—RISE

Matthew 20:18-19 (NKJV) *"Now, JESUS, going up to Jerusalem, took the twelve disciples aside on the road and said to them, Behold, we are going up to Jerusalem, and the Son of Man will be betrayed to the chief priests and to the scribes; and they will condemn Him to death, and deliver Him to the Gentiles to mock and to scourge and to crucify. And the third day He will rise again."*

❖ Emerge—It's time to come up or get up!

When examining the word RISE, it is to move from a lower position to a higher one. RISE also mean to get up from lying, sitting, kneeling, or to get out of bed. In addition, RISE means to be restored to life.

In Christian belief, the birth, death, and resurrection of Christ JESUS are key in understanding Salvation. Because without the RISE—the crucifixion would have been just an execution. The good news is that by faith, Christ did RISE from the dead, ascended to Heaven, and is seated at the right hand of the Heavenly Father with all the power to give us the ability to RISE Also.

As Believers, we can be resurrected out of any dead situation in our lives! Even now, I personally still live by the wisdom words my grandmother instilled in me as a child which was to know this: *"If you are still dealing with a situation or an illness after 3 days, then use that as a sign that it is time to RISE again! Because if CHRIST rose upon the 3rd day, GOD has ensured that you can too!"* --- wisdom words from Mable Roy Boston

PRAYER:
Thank you LORD for your love that has been displayed for me throughout my life. As I continue to grow in my spiritual walk with you, I am confident in knowing that you are with me & equips me through anything---to RISE again! In JESUS Name—Amen!

MY NOTES:

_____
_____
_____
_____
_____
_____
_____
_____
_____
_____
_____
_____
_____
_____
_____
_____
_____

MY PRAYER:

_____
_____
_____
_____
_____
_____
_____
_____
_____
_____
_____
_____
_____
_____
_____

Day 69—EXPECTATION

Acts 3:5 (NKJV) *"So he gave them his attention, expecting to receive something from them."*

❖ Expect the best!

When examining the word EXPECTATION, it means having a strong belief that something will happen or will be the case in the future. EXPECTATION also means a strong anticipation.

As children, our EXPECTATION of how much fun and excitement that was going to happen before a birthday celebration or during the Holiday season was the start of creating great anticipation. As adults, our EXPECTATIONS can be clouded with doubt and anxiety due to allowing past disappointments or experiences to distort our minds. Consequently, the root of the issue was usually in *whom* or *what* we placed our EXPECTATION.

With that said, let us begin to place our EXPECTATION in GOD and not other people, places, or things. Once done, we can then EXPECT the best and leave the rest up to GOD.

PRAYER:
Thank you LORD for the spirit of EXPECTATION. Ignite my anticipation to continue to fuel my EXPECTATION as I place my prayer requests in your hands. For I believe GOD and EXPECT GOD. In JESUS Name—Amen!

EXPECTATION

MY NOTES:

_____
_____
_____
_____
_____
_____
_____
_____
_____
_____
_____
_____
_____
_____

EXPECTATION

MY PRAYER:

_____
_____
_____
_____
_____
_____
_____
_____
_____
_____
_____
_____
_____
_____

Day 70—CAPACITY

Mark 4:40 (KVJ) *"And he said unto them, Why are ye so fearful? How it is that ye have no faith?"*

❖ Increase your CAPACITY to Believe GOD!

When examining the word CAPACITY, it means fully occupying the available area or space; CAPACITY also means the maximum amount that something can contain or produce.

Your true level of belief is shown in your actions and is heard in your words. Let's explore more.

GOD's word in Isaiah 55:11 says: *"So shall my word be that goes forth out of my mouth; It shall not return to Me void, but it shall accomplish what I please, and it shall prosper in the thing for which I sent it."*

With that said—Ask yourself:
1. Do you really take GOD at his WORD?
2. What are your actions showing?
3. What are you saying regarding the matter—It is the same as what GOD says about it?

No matter how great the storm intensity may be in your situation or circumstances—continue to persist to increase your CAPACITY to believe GOD!

PRAYER:
Thank you LORD for being GOD who continues to increase my CAPACITY to believe in all areas of my life. As I stay connected to GOD and trust GOD to do accordingly to the living, written and spoken WORD of GOD, help my unbelief. In JESUS Name—Amen!

CAPACITY

MY NOTES:

_____
_____
_____
_____
_____
_____
_____
_____
_____
_____
_____
_____
_____
_____
_____

CAPACITY

MY PRAYER:

_____
_____
_____
_____
_____
_____
_____
_____
_____
_____
_____
_____
_____
_____

Day 71—AS IS

Isaiah 1:18 (NKJV) *"Come now, and let us reason together, says the LORD. Though your sins are like scarlet, They shall be as white as snow; Though they are red like crimson, They shall be as wool."*

❖ Deal with the Real

When examining the word phrase AS-IS, it is the state that something is in at the present time. AS-IS also means accepting something in its present existing condition without modification or repair.

One of the great things about GOD as Creator is that GOD foreknew each of us. GOD already knew and knows what we do well, and what we don't—AS IS. GOD also knows all the good, bad, and the ugly that is sin within us. GOD alone has the capability to cleans us and change us to be the good, great, and excellent versions of ourselves that has been already destined.

To experience the transformation that is our destiny, we must seek GOD and come to HIM—AS IS!

PRAYER:
Thank you LORD for being faithful and just to forgive and clean us from all unrighteousness. For those GOD foreknew GOD also predestined to be conformed to the image of Christ. Continue to transform us to be more Christ like. In JESUS Name—Amen!

AS-IS

MY NOTES:

_____
_____
_____
_____
_____
_____
_____
_____
_____
_____
_____
_____
_____
_____
_____
_____

AS-IS

MY PRAYER:

_____
_____
_____
_____
_____
_____
_____
_____
_____
_____
_____
_____
_____

Day 72—EXCELLENCE

2 Corinthians 4:7 (NKJV) *"But we have this treasure in earthen vessels, that the excellence of the power may be of GOD and not of us."*

❖ Evidence of Excellence

When examining the word EXCELLENCE, it is the quality of being outstanding or extremely good. EXCELLENCE also means brilliant.

EXCELLENCE is a way we best reflect the character of GOD. EXCELLENCE is a standard to strive for daily in all that we set out to do. Although we may fall short of this standard, having a mind-set to operate with a spirit of EXCELLENCE is an attribute worth attaining.

PRAYER:
Thank you LORD, O LORD how EXCELLENT is your name in all the earth! All that GOD does reflect EXCELLENCE. May my life be a reflection of the EXCELLENCE of GOD for the glory of GOD! In JESUS Name—Amen!

MY NOTES:

_____
_____
_____
_____
_____
_____
_____
_____
_____
_____
_____
_____
_____
_____
_____
_____

EXCELLENCE

MY PRAYER:

_____
_____
_____
_____
_____
_____
_____
_____
_____
_____
_____
_____
_____
_____

Day 73—COST

Luke 14:28-29a (NKJV) *"For which of you, intending to build a tower, does not sit down first and count the cost, whether he has enough to finish it—lest after he has laid the foundation, and is not able to finish.."*

❖ Is it worth it?

When examining the word COST, it is the effort, loss, or sacrifice necessary to achieve or obtain something. COST also means an amount that must be paid or spent to buy or acquired something.

GOD has created us in his image but has given us free will to make choices. What we choose has consequences good or bad--whether seen or unseen, whether immediate or delayed.

So, before we react, respond, or just choose to do something we all should *pause for the cause* and weigh the COST. One does not have to be an expert in accounting or even good in math to do a COST-benefit analysis. A COST-benefit analysis is simply answering the following question = Is it worth it??

PRAYER:
Thank you GOD for paying the full price for my life. As I reflect on the COST, help me to constantly seek GOD's will, GOD's word, and GOD's way so that I can pursue to honor and glorify GOD in all that I do. In JESUS Name—Amen!

COST

MY NOTES:

_____
_____
_____
_____
_____
_____
_____
_____
_____
_____
_____
_____
_____
_____
_____
_____

COST

MY PRAYER:

_____
_____
_____
_____
_____
_____
_____
_____
_____
_____
_____
_____
_____

Day 74—CALL

Psalms 145:18 (NKJV) *"The LORD is near to all who call upon Him, to all who call upon Him in truth."*

❖ Who will you call?

When examining the word CALL, it means to cry out in order to summon someone or attract their attention. CALL also means to address or refer to someone by a specific name, title, or endearment. In addition, CALL means a decision, judgement, or prediction.

Technology advancements on phones allow us to utilize a 3 in 1 featured package that consist of caller-ID, call-waiting, and 3-way conference calling as features on our phones. These features have the capability to show us who is calling before you answer, be notified that another person is trying to contact you, while already on a CALL, as well as the ability to connect both callers at once. It only takes having one phone equipped with the features to take full advantage of their uses.

GOD is a 3 in 1 also. Think about it – The Heavenly Father, The Son (Anointed One) and Holy Spirt provides a full featured package that can and will equip *whosoever* with *whatever* is needed according to GOD's plan. GOD knows who you are, what is needed, and is ready to connect with you to equip you. If you have not yet called upon GOD lately, or answered the CALL from GOD—What's the hold up?

PRAYER:
Thank you LORD for your gifts and the call you have placed upon my life. May I come to know and operate in each gift and walk worthy of the CALL upon my life. In JESUS Name—Amen!

CALL

MY NOTES:

_____
_____
_____
_____
_____
_____
_____
_____
_____
_____
_____
_____
_____
_____
_____

CALL

MY PRAYER:

_____
_____
_____
_____
_____
_____
_____
_____
_____
_____
_____
_____
_____
_____

Day 75—WEARY

Galatians 6:9 (KJV) *"And let us not be weary in well doing: for in due season we shall reap, if we faint not."*

❖ Hang in there!

When examining the word WEARY, it means feeling or showing tiredness, especially as a result of excessive exertion or lack of sleep. WEARY also means to become fatigued, drained, or bored with. In addition, WEARY means to be reluctant to see or experience any more of a thing.

Anytime we stay the course on a goal we have set out to achieve, we may grow WEARY in the process. Seek GOD for the strength needed to continue onward. There will be an appointed set time for the change to come or the expected thing to manifest. GOD has precise timing in all things!

Keep striving in obedience my friend – due season is up ahead!

PRAYER:
Thank you LORD for leading, guiding, and directing me in the way I should go and the things I am to do. Although there are some WEARY days and periods of times, I continue to press forward to take refuge in you when WEARY to receive the strength and stamina need to continue the journey. In JESUS Name—Amen!

WEARY

MY NOTES:

_____
_____
_____
_____
_____
_____
_____
_____
_____
_____
_____
_____
_____
_____
_____
_____

WEARY

MY PRAYER:

_____
_____
_____
_____
_____
_____
_____
_____
_____
_____
_____
_____
_____
_____
_____

DAY 76—PURIFY

Malachi 3:2-3 (GW) *"But who will be able to endure the day he comes? Who will be able to survive on the day he appears? He is like a purifying fire and like a cleansing soap. He will act like refiner and purifier of silver. He will purify Levi's sons and refine them like gold and silver. Then they will bring acceptable offerings to the LORD."*

❖ Turn up the heat!

When examining the word PURIFY, it means to remove contaminants from. PURIFY also mean to clean and disinfect. In addition, PURIFY means to refine by removing unwanted elements.

In the purification process, the raw metal is heated with fire until it melts. Without this heating and melting, there could be no purification. As the impurities are separated off the top, the reflection of the refiner appears on the pure surface.

As we allow GOD to purify us, HIS reflection should become more and more clearer to others around us.

PRAYER:
Thank you LORD that you uphold me even when the process PURIFIES me. For when I pass through the waters, GOD is with me. When I go through the rivers those rivers will not overflow me, and when I walk through the fires of opposition, I will not be burned nor consumed because you are the LORD—my GOD, the Holy One. In JESUS name—Amen!

PURIFY

MY NOTES:

_____
_____
_____
_____
_____
_____
_____
_____
_____
_____
_____
_____
_____
_____
_____
_____

PURIFY

MY PRAYER:

_____
_____
_____
_____
_____
_____
_____
_____
_____
_____
_____
_____
_____
_____
_____

Day 77—FEAR

Isaiah 41:10 (NIV*)** *"So do not fear, for I am with you; do not be dismayed, for I am your GOD. I will strengthen you and help you; I will uphold you up with my righteous right hand."*

❖ What are you afraid of?

When examining the word FEAR, it is an unpleasant emotion caused by the belief that someone or something is dangerous, likely to cause pain, or a threat. FEAR also mean to be afraid. In addition, FEAR mean to regard with reverence and awe.

There may be many fears that people have in life, and although it may be natural to *experience* FEAR, do understand that GOD does not want us *to live* in FEAR. When we encounter things that are out of our control, comfort zones or things that literally scares us—FEAR can come upon us.

According to www.guidelines.org commentary on FEAR it states we should practice instinctively to turn to GOD when we are afraid and simply *"make it your first step to ask GOD, 'I am afraid, what should I do? When we are afraid, turn toward GOD and put our focus on HIM. Shift our eyes away from the things that make us afraid and be consumed by GOD and what HE is well able to do. GOD then does the work of answering us and delivering us from our FEARS."*

Have NO FEAR! GOD is always near!

PRAYER:
Thank you GOD for comforting me and protecting me in the mist of situations that causes FEAR. As I realize that trying to be unafraid is not always easy. However, when I shift my focus to GOD and know that GOD is a protector, provider, and deliverer, then I can rest assured that you GOD are with me doing just that! For GOD has not given me the spirit of fear, but of power, and of love, and of a sound mind. In JESUS Name— Amen!

FEAR

MY NOTES:

_____
_____
_____
_____
_____
_____
_____
_____
_____
_____
_____
_____
_____
_____
_____
_____

FEAR

MY PRAYER:

_____
_____
_____
_____
_____
_____
_____
_____
_____
_____
_____
_____
_____
_____
_____

Day 78—STORM

Mark 4:37a (NIV) "There arose a great storm..."

❖ Peace or Panic?

When examining the word STORM, it is a violent disturbance of the atmosphere with strong winds and usually rain, thunder, lighting, or snow. STORM also mean a tumultuous reaction; an uproar or controversy. In addition, STORM means to move angrily or forcefully in a specific direction or to suddenly attack and capture.

There are times when we may feel caught up in the STORMs of life and question whether GOD is even aware of the turmoil we are facing. Sometimes we may even find that the STORM that is raging is not necessary *around us* but may be *actually within* us. Regardless of what kind of wind, hail, lightening, dust, snow, rain, or even doubt STORM you may be encountering, GOD is well able to calm it, provide the needed resolve and bring us peace.

PRAYER:
Thank you LORD that you are my protector and shelter for any STORM that may come my way or cross my path. GOD is always aware of any struggles, dangers, and overwhelming odds that may have arose as a STORM to cause devastation and damage. But having GOD as my refuge, all chaos is transformed into calm—At thy word Oh LORD! Peace be still. In JESUS Name—Amen!

STORM

MY NOTES:

_____
_____
_____
_____
_____
_____
_____
_____
_____
_____
_____
_____
_____
_____
_____

STORM

MY PRAYER:

_____
_____
_____
_____
_____
_____
_____
_____
_____
_____
_____
_____

Day 79—DECEIVE

Matthew 24:4 (KJV) *"And JESUS answered and said unto them, Take heed that no man deceive you."*

❖ True or False?

When examining the word DECEIVE it means to betray, mislead, or hide the truth for personal gain or an advantage. DECIEVE also means to promote a belief, concept or idea that is false. In addition, DECEIVE means to dupe, scam, trick, or con.

"Trick or Treat" is a greeting said throughout the 31st day of October, known to be Halloween day. When you really pause to hear the options given in that greeting, who really wants to be tricked verses treated? Deception is a trick or scheme used to get what one wants under false pretense. Some forms of deception include lies, omissions, exaggerations, and understatements.

So why would one DECIEVE another? According to Buller and Burgoon (1996) there are 3 categories of motivation for deception based on their Interpersonal Deception Theory which are the following:
1. Instrumental – to avoid punishment or to protect resources
2. Relational – to maintain relationships or a bond
3. Identity – to preserve "face" or the self-image

When deception occurs, The DECEIVER and the DECEIVED both are negatively impacted by the relationship in a variety of ways that includes loss of creditability of their word and actions. Therefore, it is essential to avoid being DECEIVED or a DECEIVER.

PRAYER:
Thank you LORD for being The Way, The Truth, and The Life! I pray any spirit of deception, known or unknown, that is operating in my life be exposed & eradicated and immediately replace with the Spirit of Truth. Help me to never be DECEIVED or deceptive in things I say or do as a GOD representative in worship & serving you. In JESUS Name—Amen!

DECEIVE

MY NOTES:

_____
_____
_____
_____
_____
_____
_____
_____
_____
_____
_____
_____
_____
_____
_____
_____

DECEIVE

MY PRAYER:

_____
_____
_____
_____
_____
_____
_____
_____
_____
_____
_____
_____
_____
_____

Day 80—WORRY

Matthew 6:27 (GW) *"Can any of you add a single hour to your life by worrying?"*

❖ Be anxious for no-thing

When examining the word WORRY it is to allow one's mind to dwell on difficulty or troubles. WORRY also means a state of anxiety and uncertainty over actual or potential problems.

The unknown that we face in our lives can easily stir up WORRY in us. WORRY can simply start by us entertaining "What If?" Have you found yourself entertaining these "What ifs" into a detriment of not knowing when to stop? If so, stop and begin to trust GOD for what you thought you could handle but have realized you cannot!

To stop WORRY requires a shift from fear to faith regarding anything that may be overwhelming or challenging us.

Although life does bring us uncertainties that show up as our responsibility, do not fret or WORRY – just simply be reminded to cast that care upon GOD for HE cares for you and GOD can handle whatever that care is too!

PRAYER:
Thank you GOD that you are always available to take care of people & situations that may WORRY me. Today, I choose to focus on trusting GOD to handle these things. For you GOD are well able to help whomever with whatever. In JESUS Name—Amen!

WORRY

MY NOTES:

_____
_____
_____
_____
_____
_____
_____
_____
_____
_____
_____
_____
_____
_____
_____
_____
_____

WORRY

MY PRAYER:

_____
_____
_____
_____
_____
_____
_____
_____
_____
_____
_____
_____
_____
_____

Day 81—HUNGER

Matthews 5:6 (NIV) *"Blessed are those who hunger and thirst for righteousness, for they will be filled."*

❖ What's on the menu?

When examining the word HUNGER, it is to have a strong desire or craving for. HUNGER also mean a severe lack of food. In addition, HUNGER is a feeling of discomfort or weakness caused by a lack of nourishment, coupled with the desire to eat.

One thing that many people may take for granted is having an appetite. Depending on the time of day, whether morning/noon/night one begins to HUNGER and thirst for something to fulfill the physical body as a human being. The same is true for the spiritual part of our being.

Check your appetite. What do you crave to give your spirit for needed nutrients and nourishment to grow?

PRAYER:
Thank you LORD that you are the bread of life and living waters that quinches my HUNGER and thirst. Continue to cultivate my appetite for the things of GOD and not the things of the world. In JESUS Name— Amen!

HUNGER

MY NOTES:

_____
_____
_____
_____
_____
_____
_____
_____
_____
_____
_____
_____
_____
_____
_____
_____

HUNGER

MY PRAYER:

_____
_____
_____
_____
_____
_____
_____
_____
_____
_____
_____
_____
_____
_____
_____

Day 82—GIFT

1 Peter 4:10 (NLT) *"GOD has given each of you a gift from his great variety of spiritual gifts. Use them well to serve one another."*

❖ Time, Talent, and Treasure

When examining the word GIFT, it is a thing given willingly to someone without payment; a present. GIFT also mean a natural ability or talent. GIFT also means to be endowed with.

There are talents that each of us have. We all have been given at least one or more unique GIFT as an ability to do something extremely well. Whether we consider it small or large, this GOD-given GIFT is to contribute to the betterment of mankind. Build confidence in knowing that the thing(s) you are talented at doing, GOD has entrusted you to utilize and steward that GIFTing(s) for His Glory and His service.

Choose to hone in on the GIFT(s) you have been given. Learn more and practice more so you become sought after by others because of the perfecting expertise you have in doing what you are GIFTED to do (*Proverbs 18:16*).

The GIFT(s) are part of the purpose given for your life. Thanks be to GOD for His indescribable GIFT! For GOD has given each one of us the ability to better the lives of those around us simply by what GOD has endowed upon us and created us to be and do.

PRAYER:
Thank you GOD for endowing upon each of us the grace given according to the measure of Christ's GIFT for us. Help me to recognize my own unique GIFTs and understand the importance of my purpose in utilizing my own unique GIFTs to better the lives of others by showing GOD's love. As I am in pursuit of my purpose, utilized my own unique GIFTs, for surely it shall have a great payoff for your glory and service forever, and ever Amen! In JESUS Name—Amen!

GIFT

MY NOTES:

_____
_____
_____
_____
_____
_____
_____
_____
_____
_____
_____
_____
_____
_____
_____
_____

GIFT

MY PRAYER:

_____
_____
_____
_____
_____
_____
_____
_____
_____
_____
_____
_____
_____

Day 83—DEVOTE

Colossians 4:2 (NLT) *"Devote yourselves to prayer with an alert mind and a thankful heart."*

❖ What have you dedicated lately?

When examining the word DEVOTE it is to give all or a large part of oneself, time, or resources to. DEVOTE also means to commit or dedicate.

Living a life DEVOTED to GOD is one that has been dedicated and set apart for His service. When we DEVOTE our lives to GOD, it must consist of some intimate time and closeness which allows the DEVOTED to get to know GOD on a deeper level to understand GOD. The LORD wants us fully committed not partially. If our lives are busy with other demands and activities, we ought to remove some things to ensure that we make room for GOD.

PRAYER:
Thank you LORD for the generous invitation throughout the WORD of GOD for us to DEVOTE ourselves to GOD. May my focus be intentionally on GOD and I continually desire to DEVOTE myself to GOD daily. In JESUS Name—Amen!

DEVOTE

MY NOTES:

_____
_____
_____
_____
_____
_____
_____
_____
_____
_____
_____
_____
_____
_____

DEVOTE

MY PRAYER:

_____
_____
_____
_____
_____
_____
_____
_____
_____
_____
_____
_____
_____
_____

Day 84—HONOR

Ephesians 6:2 (NKJV) *"Honor your father and mother, which is the first commandment with promise—That is may be well with you and you may live long on the earth."*

❖ Be a Vessel of HONOR

When examining the word HONOR, it means something regarded as a rare opportunity that is to be counted as a privilege and pleasure. HONOR also means to highly respect, love, and greatly esteem. In addition, HONOR also means to fulfill an obligation or keep an agreement.

The responsibility for children to HONOR their parents is one that is for a lifetime. This commandment may be sometime easy to carry out or sometimes difficult based on the parent-child relationship. Parents are far from perfect but even as adults, when we become independent, we still may need the input and insight from our parents. As the aging process continues, we may even have to swop roles and care for our parents as they did for us as children which is also a method of HONOR.

According to a teaching plan by www.susannarjala.com HONOR is a sensitive topic "to those who may have come from homes where there was a toxic environment or abuse." HONOR can still be shown even in these difficult environments by using godly wisdom in choosing to protect oneself by incorporating boundaries and distance needed from parents. Also, in these types of environments, HONOR can be shown but not allowing manipulation. At the end of the day, we all have a set of parents whether known or unknown, and/or supportive, or not that HONOR is due. Choose to pray for your parent(s) which is always an appropriate way to HONOR them.

PRAYER:
Thank you LORD for the privilege to HONOR you as GOD and the commandment with promise to HONOR my father and mother. May I always pray for my parents and HONOR them from a place of gratitude and not obligation. In JESUS Name—Amen!

HONOR

MY NOTES:

_____
_____
_____
_____
_____
_____
_____
_____
_____
_____
_____
_____
_____
_____
_____

HONOR

MY PRAYER:

_____
_____
_____
_____
_____
_____
_____
_____
_____
_____
_____
_____
_____
_____
_____

Day 85—TRUTH

1 John 1:8 (KJV) *"If we say we have no sin, we deceive ourselves, and the truth is no in us"*

❖ TRUTH be told

When examining the word TRUTH, it means real in fact and accuracy. TRUTH also means the actual state of a matter. In addition, TRUTH means reality, and actuality; The Word of GOD.

GOD's word is TRUTH. (*John 17:17*) Choose to confess GOD's WORD daily. The WORD of GOD is a weapon that can be used to break every generational curse or cycles of sin and bondage that has been entangling the life of a Believer. GOD's word is powerful and can resurrect and change any area of your life that needs reviving or renewing. The TRUTH will give you revelation that helps reveal to you the things not seen with the physical eye and helps you to understand those things that are unseen, happening behind the scenes.

GOD's word is full of grace & TRUTH. (*John 1:14*) Choose to learn your true identity of who you are IN CHRIST when you surrender your life to GOD and receive His grace and forgiveness and live by His word of TRUTH. GOD is Spirit and they that worship GOD must worship GOD in spirit and TRUTH. For GOD is seeking such to worship Him. (*John 4:23-24*)

PRAYER:
Thank you GOD for being the Spirit of TRUTH. Let the TRUTH of your WORD have free course and full reign in my life. For my true identity is revealed in Thy word where the whole TRUTH is found. In JESUS Name—Amen!

TRUTH

MY NOTES:

_____
_____
_____
_____
_____
_____
_____
_____
_____
_____
_____
_____
_____
_____
_____

TRUTH

MY PRAYER:

_____
_____
_____
_____
_____
_____
_____
_____
_____
_____
_____
_____
_____
_____

Day 86—FAMILY

1 Timothy 5:8 (NKJV) *"But if anyone does not provide for his own, and especially for those of his household, he has denied the faith. "*

❖ Family Matters

When examining the word FAMILY, it is a group of people related to one another by blood, marriage, or bond. FAMILY also means a group of related things.

The proverbial man or woman can manage their family and work by ensuring that each FAMILY member in the household feel valued, loved, and heard. This conviction should begin when the FAMILY dynamic began. As the household grows, it is important that each FAMILY member understands it is important to maintain balance in FAMILY-time, me-time, and work-time.

Respect each other's time, and when challenges arise, make a conscious effort to meet more often and schedule some FAMILY time and activities together, even if it is to merely meet at the table for a meal. Utilize that table time to go around the table for each family member to talk about their current stressor, pressures and what they need. Pray together as a FAMILY and gather ideas and resources as a FAMILY. The FAMILY dynamic and support will be amazing!

PRAYER:
Thank you LORD for my FAMILY. Although some may be near or far away, when they are needed, the FAMILY comes together to unify on one accord to handle FAMILY matters. GOD bless my FAMILY! In JESUS Name—Amen!

FAMILY

MY NOTES:

_____
_____
_____
_____
_____
_____
_____
_____
_____
_____
_____
_____
_____
_____
_____

FAMILY

MY PRAYER:

_____
_____
_____
_____
_____
_____
_____
_____
_____
_____
_____
_____
_____
_____

Day 87—HEALED

Psalms 30:2 (NKJV) *"O LORD my GOD, I cried out to You, and You healed me."*

❖ What is the remedy?

When examining the word HEALED it means to become sound or healthy again; cured. HEALED also means to alleviate distress or anguish. In addition, HEALED means to rectify or correct an undesirable situation.

There are many life experiences that may place us in need of HEALING. Experiencing hurts, disappointments, fears, unforgiveness, grief, discouragement, mental and physical traumas, are some examples, just to name a few. As we are impacted by these life experiences, we begin to search for ways to cope. But what is the true remedy for victory?

It is GOD himself. Jehovah Rophe' – I AM HEALER! There is no-thing too hard for GOD when faced with any life occurrence that wounds us. Jehovah Rophe' can HEAL *whatever, whenever, however, forever*! GOD is the master surgeon, so call upon him and began the process required to be HEALED.

PRAYER:
Thank you GOD for being Jehovah Rophe'! I pray to be HEALED in all areas of hurts, pains, deficiencies, and disappointments that have damaged me internally or externally. Because you are God that HEALS me, I walk into my HEALING in triumphant victory! In JESUS Name— Amen!

HEALED

MY NOTES:

_____
_____
_____
_____
_____
_____
_____
_____
_____
_____
_____
_____
_____
_____
_____

HEALED

MY PRAYER:

_____
_____
_____
_____
_____
_____
_____
_____
_____
_____
_____
_____
_____
_____

Day 88—DELIVERED

Psalms 34:19 (KJV) *"Many are the afflictions of the righteous, But the LORD delivers him out of them all."*

❖ What is your hang up or stumbling block?

When examining the word DELIVERED, it means to move out of or save someone from a painful or bad experience. DELIEVERED also means to achieve or produce something that has been promised. In addition, DELIVERED means to birth.

GOD has the power to DELIVER us from any afflictions that we are facing. If some of the same old problems, the same old struggles, and the same old habits, same people, actions, thoughts, and unhealthy pattern of behaviors keep coming back time and again in your life, GOD wants you to be DELIVERED.

GOD wants us delivered so that we can do what Luke 1:74-75 says: *"That HE would grant unto us, that we being DELIVERED out of the hands of our enemies—might serve HIM—without fear, in holiness and righteousness before HIM, all the days of our life."* If we desire to be DELIVERED we have a responsibility to ask for and receive DELIVERANCE.

DELIVERANCE is available but one must want to be DELIVERED. Obedience to GOD's word, will, and way is a requirement to be DELIVERED. For DELIVERANCE comes from the LORD.

PRAYER:
Thank you LORD that deliverance is available because it was made available to us all through the redeeming blood of Christ! The price has already been paid and criteria has been met for us to be set free, healed and DELIVERED from all unrighteousness, evil, sin, afflictions and bondages. I desire to walk in total liberty knowing that GOD who has begun a good work in me shall complete it! DELIVER me LORD! In JESUS Name—Amen!

DELIVERED

MY NOTES:

_____
_____
_____
_____
_____
_____
_____
_____
_____
_____
_____
_____
_____
_____
_____
_____

DELIVERED

MY PRAYER:

_____
_____
_____
_____
_____
_____
_____
_____
_____
_____
_____
_____
_____
_____
_____

Day 89—FREEDOM

2 Corinthians 3:17 (NLT) *"For the LORD is the Spirit, and where the Spirit of the LORD is, there is Freedom"*

❖ Be set free.

When examining the word FREEDOM, it means to not be under the control or power of; FREEDOM also means to not be enslaved, captive or in bondage. In addition, FREEDOM mean to not be burdened by something or someone.

While studying the teachings *Experiencing the Heart of Jesus* by Max Lucado, I learned, for one to experience FREEDOM in full, we must understand that FREEDOM does include freeing ourselves from any mental and emotional baggage that we may carry around. This baggage may consist of suitcases of guilt, duffel bags of worry, hanging bags of grief, backpacks of loneliness, hurt, and pain, a trunk full of fears, and carryon bags of doubt and unforgiveness!

When we allow our feelings, minds, and emotions to *concern* us, *worry* us, *burden* us and *weigh* us down, to experience FREEDOM, we must learn to trust GOD. Let GOD deal, heal, and fix our issues and situations because those bags & burdens were never intended for us to carry or bare.

As an affirmation to that step, I discover it stated so appropriately by the songwriter Joseph Scriven (1820-1886) in his lyrics to the song, **What A Friend We Have in JESUS** which says the following: *"What a friend we have in Jesus, All our sins and griefs to bear! What a privilege to carry, everything to GOD in prayer! Oh, what peace we often forfeit, Oh, what needless pain we bear; All because we do not carry, everything to GOD in prayer!"*

PRAYER:
Thank you LORD for paying the full cost for us to be free! FREEDOM is what we have—Christ has made us free! Who the son makes free—is free indeed! In JESUS Name—Amen!

MY NOTES:

_____
_____
_____
_____
_____
_____
_____
_____
_____
_____
_____
_____
_____
_____

FREEDOM

MY PRAYER:

_____
_____
_____
_____
_____
_____
_____
_____
_____
_____
_____
_____
_____
_____

Day 90—BLESSED!

Proverbs 10:22 (NKJV) *"The blessing of the LORD, it makes one rich, and He adds no sorrow with it."*

❖ Blessed beyond measure!

When examining the word BLESSED, it is to pronounce words to confer or invoke divine favor upon; BLESSED also means to ask GOD to look favorably upon or to endow a particular cherished thing or attribute. In addition, BLESSED also means an expression or feeling of gratitude.

To be BLESSED originates from the Spirit of GOD giving us the authority and ability in life to have Shalom (peace) of nothing lacking, missing, or broken. The original BLESSING was spoken in the bible by GOD to man and woman to be Fruitful, Multiply, Replenish, Subdue, and have Dominion (*Genesis 1:26-28*). Therefore, being BLESSED empowers us to prosper! And it is GOD who gives us the power to get wealth (*Deuteronomy 8:18*). Thus, obedience to GOD and His WORD is required.

Anything that GOD grants to you according to GOD's WORD, will, purpose, plans, and promises will not overwhelm you even when given in overflow. Nonetheless, GOD stewardship will be necessary to accomplish the things of GOD and those things GOD desires for your own enjoyment.

As you live BLESSED, take a moment and always be reminded of this: *"The earth is the LORD's and the fullness thereof, the world and those who dwell therein"* (*Psalms 24:1*). GOD is the creator & owner of simply everything! Yes—it all! So, seek GOD and stay obedient accordingly.

PRAYER:
Thank you GOD for I am BLESSED! I continue to fully live BLESSED according to the WORD of GOD in Deuteronomy Chapter 28. And all these BLESSINGS shall come upon me in overflow because I obey the voice of the LORD my GOD! BLESSED when I come in and BLESSED when I go out. LORD continue to open unto me GOD's good treasure from heaven and BLESS all the work I do for GOD's glory and greater glory! In JESUS Name—Amen!

BLESSED!

MY NOTES:

_____
_____
_____
_____
_____
_____
_____
_____
_____
_____
_____
_____
_____
_____
_____

BLESSED!

MY PRAYER:

_____
_____
_____
_____
_____
_____
_____
_____
_____
_____
_____
_____

Call of Salvation:

If after reading this devotional you desire to receive the Gift of Salvation that GOD offers so you can start a personal relationship with GOD, you can do so right now!

John 3:16-17 (NIV) *"For GOD so loved the world that he gave his one begotten Son, that whosoever believeth in him should not perish but have everlasting (eternal) life. For GOD sent not his Son into the world to condemn the world; but the world through him might be saved."*

The WORD of GOD instructs you to do the following:

Roman 10:8-13 (NIV) *"The word is near you; it is in your mouth and in your heart, that is the message concerning faith that we proclaim: If you declare with your mouth, JESUS is LORD, and believe in your heart that GOD raised him from the dead, you will be saved. For it is with your heart that you believe and are justified, and it is with your mouth that you profess your faith and are saved."*

If you believe and confess the above – You are NOW SAVED!

I am proud of you to have made one of the best decisions of your Life! Your NEXT STEPS will be to get a Bible and seek to find a version of translation that you can easily understand and practically apply it to your life. Read the word of GOD, Pray, and Worship – stay consistent and you will be amaze of the LIFE CHANGE that will take place in you and for you as you continue to do so! Also find a local church or ministry that you can connect with in-person or online so that you can be surrounded by other Believers who can help you grow in your faith walk with GOD. You will need that support as you navigate through life as a Believer. Also begin to set out devoted time with GOD, just as you did for **Enough Time**!

Welcome to the Family!

Keep Praying for me because I am praying for you!

Much Love!

--AB

References:

Unless otherwise noted all scriptures are from the following translations of the HOLY BIBLE:

King James Version (**KJV**), New King James Version (**NKJV**), New Living Translation (**NLT**), English Standard Version (**ESV**), New International Version (**NIV**), American Standard Version (**ASV**), Good News Translation (**GNT**), God Word (**GW**)

Apple Siri - iPhone
Nelson's Quick Reference Bible Concordance
You Version – Holy Bible App (scriptures and bible plans)
WritingExplain.org
Dictionary.com
Merriam-Webster.com
Microsoft Encarta Dictionary
Microsoft Thesaurus
Wikipedia
Cambridge Dictionary
Dr. Bob the drugless doctor www.drugless.doctor.com
The Holy Spirit by Billy Graham
What You Need to Know about The Holy Spirit by Max Anders
Teachings from Bishop Clarence E. McClendon
Teachings from Bishop TD Jakes
Teachings from Apostle Jerome Nelson

Made in the USA
Middletown, DE
19 May 2023

30595431R00110